DO SOMETHING WITH THIS BOOK

THINK

SHARE

NOTE

PRESENT

APPLY

SUBSCRIBE

TAKE ON TRIP

BOOKMARK

REFLECT

DISCUSS

HAVE A CUP

FOR OTHERS

Other books by Leandro Herrero:

The Trouble with Management (out of print)

The Leader with Seven Faces
Finding your own ways of practicing leadership in today's organization

New Leaders Wanted: Now Hiring!
12 kinds of people you must find, seduce, hire and create a job for

Viral Change™
The Alternative To Slow, Painful and Unsuccessful Management of Change in Organizations

Disruptive Ideas. 10+10+10=1000
The maths of Viral Change™ that transform organizations

Ideas Rompedoras
Las reglas del Cambio Viral para transformer organizaciones

Homo Imitans - The art of social infection: Viral Change™ in action

However: Work Could Be Remarkable

Soon to be available:

The Little Book of Big Change. Universal rules for change makers

Unplugged. Organizations under new management

Homo Imitans (second edition)

Exotics on the payroll. The anthropology of life in organizations

Victims or agents? The modern choices of employee engagement

All books are available from Amazon, Barnes and Noble, Blackwell, Waterstones, Books Etc. and many other bookshops.

For book enquiries and bulk orders please contact:

meetingminds@thechalfontproject.com

First published in 2020 by: **Meetingminds**

Meetingminds is a division of The Chalfont Project.

MEETINGMINDS
PUBLISHING

The Chalfont Project Ltd, Charter Building, Charter Place, Uxbridge, United Kingdom UB8 1JG

Email: **meetingminds@thechalfontproject.com**

ISBN 978-1-905776-18-4

A CIP catalogue record for this title is available from the British Library.

The
Flipping
Point

The Flipping Point

DEPROGRAMMING MANAGEMENT

Leandro Herrero

MEETINGMINDS
PUBLISHING

"The curse of modernity is that we are increasingly populated by a class of people who are better at explaining than understanding, or better at explaining than doing."

Nassim Nicholas Taleb, *Skin in the Game: Hidden Asymmetries in Daily Life*

"A desk is a dangerous place from which to view the world."

John le Carré

"To err is human, to blame it on someone else shows management potential."

Anonymous

Most of the boldness, benign irreverence, and flipping uncompromising that are commonly attributed to my character are in fact largely induced, incited and stimulated by Caroline, co-founder of The Chalfont Project, and my wife.

Caroline always provides me with a map and safe passage to that Socratic territory of 'an unexamined life is not worth living'. Had Socrates met Caroline, he would have had to push the tone a little bit more on the ambitious side.

To her, this book.

And then to Tom and Aisling, who thanks to her have at least 50% Irish DNA. And an Irish passport. God bless the Republic in these flipping Brexit days.

Go raibh maith agat

Index:

The Prologue

I am an organization architect. That's my job. I am a practitioner. I practice first, then write about it.

I'll be blunt. I want to reach a flipping point in the trend for adopting absurd management ideas. Soon, please. We are working in tunnel vision mode through the lenses of a particular worldview, that of the Anglo-American enterprises and Anglo-American business schools.

This is a worldview that puts a premium on scientism and wins battles and budgets by overwhelming executives with 'data' and 'research shows'. However, in this world of ours, we are terribly casual with causality.

Causality has never been a great preoccupation of management thinking. One can simply stitch two activities, two management practices, two Best Practices together, create a link, and get away with murder, with nobody challenging it. Also add a label such as 'research from McKinsey' or 'published in the Harvard Business Review' (at best a light, entertaining magazine) and you can guarantee two things: it will

never be validated and you will have a place for ever in the common pool of management wisdom, and maybe even a quote in an MBA class.

Prestigious business schools, academics and Big Management Consulting firms produce daily pieces of 'research' that are mere journalistic accounts of what 100 or 300 CEOs say. These CEOs repeat what they have read in the publications of the same business schools, academic institutions and Big Management Consulting firms. The circle of that colossal groupthink is alive and well. The bars in Davos are having a good time. These are also, no wonder, the same consulting firms that have skilfully and expensively worked with organizations for many years, always leaving them fully prepared for their past.

Most management thinking today, established as the norm, is unidirectional in cause-effect. It is populated by a collection of post-hoc fallacies and cognitive biases. For example, we are told that high employee engagement creates very successful organizations, but never told that very successful organizations create high employee engagement. We are told that excellent businesses have in common, 5 characteristics of, or 7 steps of, or 5 strong principles. We are never told why many failed organizations also had the same 5 characteristics of, or the 7 steps of, or those 5 strong principles. Leadership 'research' is even worse. We are told that a bunch of exemplary organizations, top of something, best in some sort of class, the 'Big List', have in common a kind of leadership that is inclusive, supportive, authentic, people centred and something else. Nobody dares to say that similar leadership traits can be found in organizations that did not make that List. Or any list at all. Or have disappeared in the last 10 years.

To avoid seriously 'looking inside' and under the microscope, (which could be embarrassing), we have diverted the attention to the future. We have entire business school departments and expert gurus cum-book-and-podcast, talking about 'the future of work', whilst the present is suffocated with nonsense (including reams of PowerPoints about the future). Our real and present danger is not a future of robots and AI, it is the real and present danger of current bullshit.

I am far from immune to the contagion, but I have spent my 20 years as an organizational architect (post time as a senior manager in those organizations,

post clinical psychiatrist) using that chronic exposure to create antibodies. These 200 tweet-sized vignettes, twitter-on-paper, which can be read in no particular order, are my coin flipping, my looking at the other side of things.

There is no science behind it. Pure praxis. I have not interviewed 1000 CEOs or visited the 'sexy-of-the-month' companies, today described as models of something. I am sharing my views from my praxis, not because I believe I am in possession of the truth, but because I want to invite everybody to the Mother of All Call Outs! The sun does not circle the earth, Father Christmas can't fly, 'employees are our most important assets' is a nonsensical platitude, top leadership power is overrated, business case studies give journalism a bad name, and diversity is not the number of women on the Board.

I am also overdoing it on the Nespresso.

1.

PEOPLE'S LOYALTY IS TO THE TRIBE FIRST (FUNCTION, TEAM, PRODUCT, BRAND), THEN TO THE LARGER VISION. THE LATTER MAY NOT EVEN HAPPEN AT ALL. TO PRETEND THAT ALL EMPLOYEES MUST HAVE UNEQUIVOCAL LOYALTY TO THE ULTIMATE GOALS OF THE FIRM IS A BAD IDEA ORIGINATED IN THE NORTH KOREAN BUSINESS SCHOOL.

2.

My rule of thumb. Value systems 'on the wall' are more likely to denote a scarcity of them than a serious aspiration. Only organizations which have poor teamwork, put teamwork as a value on the wall. The ones with great teamwork don't bother. Same for integrity. Ditto for almost anything. The public display of a company's value system may be the most accurate diagnosis of its deficiencies, not its real aspirational values.

3.

Peer-to-peer networks are dynamite. Teams are ground transportation, not Formula 1.

4.

'The system will prevent itself from solving the problems it creates'. If you remember this, then you'll be able to understand the tension between wanting to improve a system and the system itself saying to you 'over my dead body'. It's the organization's autoimmune system that gets in the way.

5.

EMPOWERMENT WITHOUT
SKIN IN THE GAME IS
PASSING THE MONKEY
(AND THERE IS A WHOLE
ZOO IN ORGANIZATIONS).
IF YOU EMPOWER OTHERS,
BUT THERE IS NO RISK TO
YOU IN DOING IT, YOU ARE
JUST PASSING THE BUCK.
YOUR EMPOWERMENT
SUCKS. IT IS NOT WORTH
THE NAME, NO MATTER
HOW GOOD YOU OR THE
ONE EMPOWERED FEEL
ABOUT IT. AT BEST IT IS
PURE DELEGATION. AT
WORST DISHONESTY.

6.

Trust, engagement and happiness are outcomes. If you treat them like inputs, you'll never get them. You can't inject trust. We have not figured out yet how to put trust in the water supply of the organization. You do things that make people feel trusted. Same for happiness, engagement, pride. It's what comes out, not what goes in.

7.

Complaints about lack of X in organizations only take place when there is already a lot of X around. To complain about a lack of diversity and inclusion you have to already be reasonably diverse and inclusive. Those who have zero of it, don't have the means or power to even complain, or don't even have the capacity to question whether they need it. People who complain that their identity is not respected may be in an environment in which identity is respected well above average.

8.

There is only one strategy test: what will you tell the children? Try this: Son, I got up every day and went to the office to maximise shareholder value. I also participated in lots of Lean Teams. Ah, and I was an agile employee. In my time, our employee engagement scores went up from 4.5 to 7. Just try. Rehearse this by saying it to yourself in the mirror. Yes, what will we tell the children? That's probably the only question that matters.

9.

'Act as if you were an owner', is a company philosophy and type of message to staff which should only be accepted if bonuses and stock options are included. Otherwise, it is one of those bad jokes floating around organizations and sanctioned by Harvard Business School and Amazon's Principles. This management absurdity and MBA speak is unfortunately still alive and well.

10.

PEOPLE WHO ASK 'WHAT IS IN IT FOR ME' SHOULD NEVER BE GIVEN AN ANSWER. IF THEY CANNOT FIGURE IT OUT FOR THEMSELVES, THEY HAVE A BIG PROBLEM. NOT YOU. TEMPTING AS IT MAY BE, NEVER ANSWER THAT.

11.

THERE ARE PEOPLE WITH WHOM YOU SHARE A PROBLEM AND YOU ALWAYS END UP WITH TWO.

12.

The greatest liability of people 'who have done this before' is that they have done that before. Same for people with great experience who may just have the same single experience repeated for 30 years.

13.

CHARISMATIC
LEADERSHIP
IS MOSTLY
DENIGRATED
BY PEOPLE WHO
THEMSELVES
POSSESS THE
CHARISMA OF
A FISH CAKE.

14.

COMPANIES THAT
HAVE BECOME
PROFICIENT AT
SOLVING PROBLEMS,
TEND TO CREATE
MORE PROBLEMS
(TO BE SOLVED).
THEY NEED TO FEED
THEIR PROFICIENCY.
PROBLEM SOLVING
AS A COMPETENCE
CLIMAX IS A BAD IDEA.
YOU'LL SOLVE LOTS,
WILL CREATE MANY
MORE, AND WILL NEVER
BUILD ANYTHING.

15.

People often say, organizations have a big communication problem. I agree. But the problem is not that they communicate too little, but that they communicate too much. Channels are saturated. People don't distinguish between signal and noise anymore. The greater the communicating, the bigger the noise. Several corporate functions and their initiatives are competing for airtime, and it's only Wednesday afternoon. If you want to improve communication, want to have a healthy communication strategy, communicate less.

16.

YOU ARE YOUR CALENDAR. DON'T TELL ME YOUR TITLE, SHOW ME YOUR OUTLOOK CALENDAR.

17.

You can't manage a company culture via an employee survey score, up and down, yoyo style. You can't manage an infection by lowering the fever. Most serious people understand that, but they also keep doing employee surveys and paralysing the organization afterwards to 'fix the deficiencies'. Entire company culture efforts have been hijacked by numbers in a score system. That kind of employee engagement emperor has no clothes.

18.

The worst leaders I have encountered in organizations are the ones who trumpet their unique humanity, or unique Christianity, or unique values. The more they say that, the more dangerous they are. Leaders with solid values don't go around saying 'these are my solid values'.

19.

TOP LEADERSHIP ROLE
MODELLING IS OVERRATED.
IT'S HISTORY'S EQUIVALENT
OF THE GREAT MAN THEORY,
ALWAYS ONE BEHIND EVENTS.
MOST PEOPLE DON'T ARRIVE
AT 09:00 IN THE CAR PARK
WONDERING HOW THE TOP
LEADERS WILL BEHAVE THAT
DAY. MOST DON'T CARE, SORRY.
THEIR ROLE MODELS ARE
THEIR PEERS. WHAT SHAPES
BEHAVIOURS IS WHAT YOU
COPY EVERY DAY FROM YOUR
IMMEDIATE ENVIRONMENT.
IN ROLE MODELLING, PEER-TO-
PEER ONE, TOP LEADERSHIP NIL.

20.

The ultimate role of the leader is to lose control. The more control you lose, the more you actually have. If you can't afford to lose control 'because it may cause chaos', the problem is you. In the best case, you don't have the right structure behind you. So, the problem is you. Or you inherited it. Still you. In the worst case, you have created that structure. The problem is you big time. Leadership development equals bits of control I want to lose per month.

21.

THE BEST QUESTION IS THE ONE THAT HAS NO ANSWER. THIS IS A BIG PROBLEM IN ORGANIZATIONS BECAUSE WE HAVE A SUPERMARKET OF READY-MADE ANSWERS WAITING FOR ANY POSSIBLE QUESTIONS. 'ANSWERS ON DEMAND' SEEM TO BE IN THE FRONTISPIECE OF MANY CORPORATE GROUPS.

22.

IF YOU HAVE A LOT OF ANALYTICAL PEOPLE WHO CAN DISSECT AN ELEPHANT AND HAVE BECOME PROFICIENT IN ANYTHING TO DO WITH ITS PARTS, GOOD LUCK WHEN YOU HAVE A REAL ELEPHANT IN FRONT OF YOU BUT YOU HAVE ONLY COMMISSIONED ALL POSSIBLE MARKET RESEARCH ON TRUNKS.

23.

BUSINESS CASE
STUDIES ARE A BAD
FORM OF JOURNALISM.
THEY GIVE JOURNALISM
A BAD NAME.

24.

**Finance is soft, culture
is hard. If you have not
discovered it yet, you need
to end that sabbatical
on Mars soon.**

Passion is overrated. Most of the time, it is hard work. Then, people become passionate about it. Passion as an output is brilliant. Passion as an input is, at best, 'suspended judgement'. You never know what a bunch of passionate arsonists may do.

26.

I am very sorry to have to bring bad news to you: there is no 'They'. As in 'They won't like it', or 'They don't listen' or 'They are the problem'. 'They' is an organizational Goddess who seems to have incredible power. But, after years of searching for 'They, the Goddess', I have come to the conclusion that she does not exist. There is no 'They'. Acknowledging this has been equally stressful and liberating.

27.

Culture is what happens when compliance leaves the room.

28.

We have blindly glorified collaboration. But collaboration is not always good. Imagine high collaboration of lazy people, terrorists, pseudo-victims, negativists, cynics, professional sceptics, defeatists, or dysfunctional members of a leadership team. In fact, anything that facilitates collaboration of them, including digital platforms and Enterprise Social Networks, is organizational self-flagellation.

29.

Individual change does not precede social change. By all means, 'Be the change you want to see in the world' (by the way, Gandhi never said that), but bring lots of your friends, and ask those friends to bring their friends. Individual change is not a precondition for social change. In fact, most of the time it is the other way around. There is social change, and then individuals change. But accepting this puts you on a collision course with decades of folk psychology. Very sorry if you don't like this. PS: believing in 'individual change first' provides a marvellous alibi for not starting the revolution today.

All useless or ineffective processes that seem untouchable, are in fact rituals that have nothing to do with the declared goal of the process. Rituals are rock solid. They are wholly ineffective for their official goal. Dancing around a fire does not produce rain (unless the weather forecast already said so, in which case the Shaman has an unfair competitive advantage) but it's a lot of fun, apparently. Many long-winded, idea recycling, PowerPoint-based, business planning processes lasting for months, are simply executive fire dancing (without the funny hats). It makes no sense, but we keep doing it.

31.

PROCESS JUNKIES NEED TREATMENT, NOT PROMOTION TO VP OR A DEPARTMENT FULL OF ADDICTS.

34.

Leadership is a club to which Mandela, Hitler, Mother Teresa, Mao, Obama, Tony Soprano and Pope Francis belong. This club has the most terrible admissions policy. I would not recommend it.

33.

TRUST IS NON LINEAR (EXCUSE MY LANGUAGE). USUALLY IT'S HARD OR LONG TO GAIN, BUT IT'S ALWAYS ONE SCREW UP AWAY FROM KILLING IT.

34.

THE MOST TOXIC KIND OF EMPLOYEE OR MANAGER IS THE SAVIOUR. SAVIOURS ARE WAITING TO SAVE YOU. THEY CREATE THE PROBLEMS FROM WHICH YOU NEED TO BE SAVED.

To be very effective you have to be a bit inefficient. Pure efficiency never produces innovation. No slack, no adaptation. Cutting resources to the bone is death announced. If you have optimised everything, a little hiccup will kill you, somebody said. Effectiveness on the other hand needs the space to achieve the unexpected and a much greater than planned goal. Entire reorganizations have missed that point. Big Consulting Firms don't understand this. After the 'cutting to the bone' and 'eliminating fat', the residual architecture works as a predictable piece of machinery. It's slim, post diet, post Botox, post cosmetic surgery and stupidly hopeless. But millions in consulting fees later, it has more people with the word Global on their business card.

36.

Corporate Social Responsibility (CSR) is tested everyday with employees in the corridor. How you treat employees defines your CSR score. The rest is commentary.

37.

Diversity and Inclusion start with diversity of ideas and opinions, and end with gender. Never the other way around. Diversity and Inclusion programmes in an organization in which nobody speaks up, end up with an extra couple of women in the Executive Committee, who also don't speak up.

38.

Don't read anything that starts with 'research has shown'.

39.

Stop announcing change. Change.
Then announce that it's happening.
In fact, it's broader than change.
Don't announce. Ever.
I'm going to show you a video: just show it.
Some people spend half their life
announcing the other half.

40.

Demonising hierarchy is easy and politically correct but not terribly efficient, unless you have a serious alternative. Most alternatives are simply a type of trade-off. From the hard dictatorship of the top leaders to the benign dictatorship of team leaders. From the benign dictatorship of team leaders, to the invisible dictatorship of the pseudo-democratic 'we don't have managers here'. Then, the power to those who shout more. Then, back to 'I think we need good leaders'. Then, back to some sanitised hierarchical structure. Then up again. It's merry-go-round management. The only question is when is best to stop the music for a while. Where the best trade-off is.

41.

A CULTURE OF SAFETY IS NOT THE SAME AS A CULTURE OF TRAINING IN SAFETY. A CULTURE OF CUSTOMER-CENTRISM IS NOT THE SAME AS A CULTURE OF LOTS OF TRAINING IN CUSTOMER-CENTRISM. A CULTURE OF SALES ORIENTATION IS NOT THE SAME AS A CULTURE OF TRAINING IN SALES MANAGEMENT. IN FACT, CULTURES WITH OBSESSIVE TRAINING ON SAFETY, CUSTOMER-CENTRISM, OR SALES ORIENTATION, BECOME OBSESSIVE CULTURES OF OBSESSIVE TRAINING. PROBABLY THEIR KEY ASSET IS TRAINING. THEY SHOULD SELL TRAINING.

42.

AN EPIDEMIC OF
NASTINESS CAN ONLY
BE COMBATED BY A
COUNTER-EPIDEMIC OF
KINDNESS. DON'T FIGHT A
BEHAVIOURAL EPIDEMIC
FROM INSIDE. DON'T
TRY TO CONVERT NASTY
PEOPLE ONE BY ONE. USE
YOUR ENERGY TO FLOOD
THE SYSTEM WITH AS
MUCH NON-NASTINESS
AS POSSIBLE. YOUR
HOPE IS A COUNTER-
EPIDEMIC OF THE
OPPOSITE, NOT FIGHTING
FROM INSIDE. IF YOU
HAVE AN EPIDEMIC
OF INDIVIDUALISM,
DON'T FIGHT IT AT AN
INDIVIDUAL LEVEL. IT'S
A WASTE AND YOU'LL
NEVER WIN. CREATE
A COUNTER-EPIDEMIC
OF COLLABORATION
THAT TAKES OVER. IN
THE ORGANIZATION,
(BEHAVIOURAL) CHANGE
IS SOCIAL. OR IT ISN'T.

43.

In any change programme
(whatever that may mean)
the most important thing
is to know what is not for
changing. 'This will not
change', is always the best
start for a change narrative.

44.

If you have two
guys who think the
same, fire one of
them (this is not
mine, regrettably).

45.

THERE ARE ONLY 3 REASONS WHY PEOPLE DO WHAT THEY DO: BECAUSE THEY ARE TOLD TO, BECAUSE THEY WANT TO, AND BECAUSE OTHERS DO IT. IF YOU RUN THE ORGANIZATION BASED ON THE FIRST ONE, GOOD LUCK. THE IDEAL COMPANY IS ONE MADE UP OF PEOPLE WHO DO NOT NEED TO BE THERE, BUT WHO WANT TO BE. A COMPANY OF VOLUNTEERS. MAYBE IT SHOULD GO ON YOUR SCORECARD: CREATE A COMPANY OF VOLUNTEERS.

46.

Decouple influence and hierarchy. You may be high up in the hierarchy, but your influence is very limited. If you are high up in the system and wanted to unlock influence, chances are there are more powerful people than you. If you are the CEO, this is a 100% probability. Unless you suffer from egomania, my strong suggestion is that you find out about those people who have real power. The natural leaders and highly connected individuals. Forget the organization chart. The lady in the mailroom is a good start. After all, she sees a hundred times more people than you every day.

Some organizations are in
permanent rehearsal-mode.
We discuss, plan, prepare for
when we have the budget, when
the new management team is in
place, when we decide the merger,
when we fill the vacancies, when
the reorganization is done. This
ends up creating a culture that
has learnt to wait, delay, postpone.
It's never the right time to bite the
bullet. Their competence is waiting,
not preparing. The company
is a theatrical Green Room, a
sophisticated Waiting Room
populated by highly paid players.
An entity called Not Yet Inc.

48.

When the organization works as an aggregation of echo chambers (mainly team based), where people hear what they want to hear and constantly self-reinforce their beliefs, innovation is unattainable. When some of those echo chambers have 'innovation' in their title or on the business cards of their members, then the whole thing is a joke. When the leadership team is an echo chamber in itself, then the organization is fully dysfunctional, and their strategic plan belongs to Cloud Cuckoo Land. No reorganization, leadership development, change management or cultural change programme has any chance of success until and unless the echo chamber system is disrupted. For this to happen, you need to disband all teams and start again with a significant percentage of aliens in the membership (people from outside or other divisions, or with no previous experience and preconceived ideas). Otherwise echo chambering is a terminal illness.

49.

'Assume goodwill' is a good start. You may be wrong, but you will never regret starting that way.

50.

The company is not an Internal Diplomatic Service where people always act as if they are representing somebody else other than themselves. Teams are often composed of representatives (of a function, division, structure, stakeholder) or ambassadors of something, or of somebody, or of somewhere. Those teams don't have real people. Meetings run with these avatars are a bad idea.

51.

In the first 50 days of a new CEO, he should cut corporate initiatives by half. The problem is which half.

52.

Nasty, sceptical, negative, toxic people cannot be changed by rational appeal, performance management or special prayers. Only the group has the power. Transplant them to a place where the audience have no time for nonsense. You may see miracles.

53.

The 9 to 5 management language should match the after 5 language with kids and wives and husbands. That rules out 'strategic imperatives', 'leverage', 'net-net', 'bottom lines' and 'alignment'. Unless you married a CFO.

54.

'It is difficult to get a man to understand something, when his salary depends on his not understanding it'. There is hope. It's not that some people are as thick as they sound. Hardly. It's their salary, stupid. Now I get it.

55.

CULTURE IS MORE OF A LANDSCAPE AND A TAPESTRY THAN EXCEL SPREADSHEETS AND BAR CHARTS.

56.

Town Hall meetings are fireworks. Offsite meetings are corporate flash mobs. Both are fun, no doubt.

57.

CHANGE MANAGEMENT IS DEAD. IT NEEDS A FUNERAL NOT A FUNCTION.

58.

TOTAL SELF-MANAGEMENT IS ONLY PROMOTED BY PEOPLE WHO HAVE NEVER MANAGED ANYTHING, OR ARE VERY BAD AT IT, OR HAVE READ THAT BOOK.

WHY CAN HIGHLY PAID SUPREMOES OF MANAGEMENT NOT PROCESS MORE THAN 3 BOTTOM LINERS AND 3 BULLET POINTS? I SOMETIMES HAVE THIS MENTAL PICTURE OF PEOPLE WAITING FOR MOSES TO COME DOWN FROM THE MOUNTAIN WITH THE TABLET ANNOUNCING: 'I'VE GOT 10 COMMANDMENTS', AND THE JEWS SHOUTING BACK: 'PRIORITIZE! PRIORITIZE! GIVE US THE TOP THREE! THE NET-NET'! OR THE EXECUTIVE SUMMARY'. WE LIVE UNDER THE TYRANNY OF THE TOP 3.

I call 'impossible to disagree with' a condition of a statement, or a plan, or a proposal, or a set of findings, which provides great comfort for the audience but sheds little light on what to do next. Examples of 'impossible to disagree with' can be seen everywhere in the organization. They are automatically reinforced precisely by our inability to disagree with them. If this is the best quality of a supposedly new idea, ('impossible to disagree with'), get rid of it.

61.

Surveys tell you the what, almost never the why. Maybe this is why they are so popular. The why answer may be dangerous.

62.

'The Stone Age did not end because we ran out of stones; it ended because we invented new tools' (former Saudi Oil Minister). In our organizations, we are in the Era of Teams and Formal Structures. A super-sophisticated system of super-high performing teams will not take us out of our Stone Age. Most of our management thinking is full of more-of-the-same concepts but upgraded or relabelled, providing an illusion of modernity.

63.

Teamocracy
has dominated
organizational life,
but it's done.
Next please.

64.

Established management thinking is an intellectual collage: Starbucks did that, HSBC did that, Best Buy did that. A supermarket of examples to suit an argument. But, in fact, with more honesty, it should sound more like this: For creativity and genius dial 3 for Steve Jobs, for soviet culture also dial 3 for Apple (yes, the same Jobs). Dial 4 for highly valued McKinsey. Also dial 4 for the same McKinsey fiascos of Swiss and Enron.

65.

SUCCESS, IT'S NEVER THE OPPOSITE OF FAILURE. FAILURE IS NEVER THE OPPOSITE OF SUCCESS. THEY ARE DIFFERENT ROADS OCCASIONALLY CROSSING EACH OTHER.

66.

"

I can only work with people who
(1) don't take themselves too seriously,
(2) can use full sentences, (3) don't do
'small difference', (4) have unlimited
curiosity and, (5) they are faster than me.

Smoking kills, don't drink and drive, get the flu vaccination, wear the safety gear, etc. We know what to do or not to do, but this is not a guarantee of logical consequent behaviour. Lack of rational understanding is hardly the problem. Any managerial or leadership systems that rely solely on communications, awareness or skilling, the rational side of us, and have no room for the irrational, the social and the emotional, are flawed.

Innovation has to do with seeking unpredictable answers. The predictable ones are already taken by the previous innovation. That is why cohesive, high performing, fully aligned teams are very bad for innovation. We know each other so well that there is no unpredictable answer to hope for.

69.

A reason why it's so difficult to shape culture in the areas of Safety (oil and gas, transportation, engineering), or Ethics & 'Good Conduct' (banking/finance/investment) is because 'culture programmes' in those areas are entirely focused on avoiding the negative instead of reinforcing the positive: no accidents, no risk, no unethical behaviour (speaking up, more whistle blowers). But, for every energetically fought negative behaviour (avoiding bad news) there are thousands of positive ones never reinforced. All the airtime goes to the bad news, so it gets the energy and the reinforcement. It's popular thinking but makes no sense in behavioural terms. It seems to follow the rule that complaints are actionable, compliments are not. But, for every unsafe event there are thousands of safe ones. Reward safety, not avoidance of the unsafe.

70.

Bermuda Triangles in the company: flip charts, intranets, training binders, multiple inboxes, overinclusive meetings and people with 'Global' on their business card.

71.

Many long, complex and expensive reorganization projects led by Big Consulting Groups make companies fully prepared for their past.

72.

EMPLOYEES SHOULD TREAT THEIR BOSSES AS THEIR INVESTMENT FUND MANAGERS. IF THE HUMAN CAPITAL DOES NOT GROW, IT WOULD BE SENSIBLE TO CHANGE THE FUND MANAGER. OK, I MEAN LEAVE.

73.

The cost of not doing something is one of the most forgotten questions in management.

74.

'I AM UNCONDITIONALLY SUPPORTIVE AND FULLY BEHIND THE PROJECT, BUT I HAVE 3 CONCERNS.'

75.

HABITS HAVE NO MEANING, THEY CREATE IT. START WITH BEHAVIOURS, GET MEANING.

76.

We have made character,
virtue or goodness
uncomfortable terms
in the organization.
They seem to provoke
some sort of red face.
We see them as aliens
to the clinical, sanitized,
uncontaminated
management thinking
and language. We need
to bring them back,
welcome them to a
home they should never
have left. Imagine this:
hiring a leader of high
moral character. How
many people will laugh?
Why have we sterilized
management?

'A study in Harvard Business Review' and 'A new 3 star Michelin McDonald's', either at the start of a sentence, are not very promising for anything that comes after.

78.

I make my best clients restless; the others are content. The very best become friends.

79.

Some leaders distinguish themselves by their imminent irrelevance, but the problem is that, unfortunately, imminence seems to prolong itself forever.

80.

If the company is overheating and has no thermostat, every day without an explosion is pure luck. Leaders are the thermostats. Amongst other things.

81.

Do it right the
first time, but also
experiment and learn
from mistakes. Be bold
but be careful. Focus,
but have a helicopter
view. Ok, find yourself
a good therapist,
an expert on split
personality disorder
and charge it to HR.

82.

Leaders have two hats. Hat one is the hierarchical one, the one that is usually the reason to be hired or promoted. It comes with a position in the top down structure. Hat two is the one I have described as Backstage Leadership™. Hat two uses the power of hat one to create the conditions for peer-to-peer and informal networks to work, without dictating what to do, without interfering. Hat two recognises that leadership is distributed across the organization and beyond the boxes of the organization chart, the one populated by hat ones.

83.

For every piece of business advice that makes sense there is an opposite that makes equal sense. Also, give me a management assertion and I will give you a case study that forcefully proves it, and a case study that unequivocally disproves it completely. Give me an afternoon.

84.

WELCOME TO TOWNVILLE. POPULATION 350, CHURCHES 3, BARS 11, SHEEP 200, VETERINARIAN 1, BARBERS 2, TOTAL 567. IN OUR ORGANIZATIONS, LOTS OF OUR METRICS SYSTEMS ARE BUILT IN A SIMILAR WAY.

85.

When Compliance people, Quality people and Health and Safety people say 'the last thing we need is creativity or entrepreneurship' everybody laughs. That's easy. But you forget the jokes in the car park. No real conversations advance.

86.

SHOCK AND AWE
COMMUNICATION
CAMPAIGNS
DE-SCALE QUICKLY,
THEY NEVER SCALE UP.
IT'S FIREWORKS.
THEY ARE NICE.

87. RULES OF VIRAL CHANGE™

1. Communication is not change. 'Smoking kills' does not stop people smoking.

2. No revolution has been created by PowerPoint.

3. Behaviours don't like PowerPoint. They are not sent via email either. You can only attach words.

4. Change is not measured by the number of workshops.

5. Cultures are not created by training.

6. There is no change unless there is behavioural change.

7. Change behaviours, get culture. Not the other way around.

8. For culture, think social infection, behavioural warfare. Biological infection, idea infection and behavioural infection are similar.

9. Promote positive behaviours, don't give airtime to the negative. Ever.

10. When it comes to culture, peer-to-peer influence beats hierarchical influence.

11. Call-to-action is not action. Wanting to do, thinking of doing or commitment to doing are not doing.

12. Advocates and ambassadors are not enough, activists are. If you don't like the word, get over it.

13. Activism: youth-to-youth, grannies-to-grannies. Always transversal, never top down.

14. Engagement is action, not click-tivism, or like-tivism.

15. Target hubs, not the entire population.

16. Provide constant social proof of small progress (stories). Never wait for the big impact.

17. 'Nudge' if you wish, but have a plan of spread for the day after (Nudge Theory has no clue about Network Theory).

18. Disrupt silent majorities, engage with creative minorities.

19. Ruthlessly disrupt the negative perception of a localised problem that is seen as universal. Three guys whinging in a pub is not 'the programme is failing'.

20. Top leadership has power. They need to use it to support those who have even more power (peer-to-peer networks).

21. Walk the talk, in that order. Talk once you have walked. Only then is it infectious.

22. 'Authorities' are the worst campaigners.

23. Stories 'of behaviours' are the WMD (Words of Mass Diffusion).

24. Change methods tell you how to go from A to Z, never why.

25. Learn to shoot sacred cows (fast).

The best ideas in conferences come during the break. The best conference is the one structured as a very long coffee break. Maybe the best type of company is the one that functions as a long coffee break.

"

89.

Everybody agrees the strategy in the meeting room. Everybody trashes the strategy in the toilets during the break. If you want to have honest meetings, have them in the toilet. It saves months of finding the truth.

90.

The obsession with what is obviously measurable, in front of your eyes, leads inevitably to blindness to what is not in front of your eyes, what is not obviously measurable, and potentially the most important thing to track. This may sound obvious.

When recruiting,
ask for examples
of mistakes lived in
previous employments.
Hire only those who
attribute some mistakes
to themselves. No single
attribution (unsolicited
expressed), stop the
interview there.

92.

ANYTHING IN A SENTENCE BEFORE THE WORD 'BUT' IS BULLSHIT. NOT MY IDEA, UNFORTUNATELY.

93.

A POOR TOP LEADERSHIP GUARANTEES PERMISSION TO GET AWAY WITH MURDER DOWNSTREAM.

94.

Trust is key. If we don't have trust in organizations, people won't trust each other and, without trust, it's impossible to trust anything. If leaders trust, others will trust. If leaders don't trust, it's very difficult to have trust in the organization, and an organization with low trust, well, it's not very trustable. The Dalai Lama said (something about trust) and the best leaders such as (pick one) have always put trust at the top. Trust is key. (I am afraid, this is how many things sound in management books and from gurus).

95.

ELEVATOR PITCHES. NOTHING THAT NEEDS EXPLAINING IN AN ELEVATOR, IS WORTH EXPLAINING AT ALL. NOT EVEN IF YOU ARE GOING TO THE 42ND FLOOR.

96.

SOME LEADERS HAVE AN OPEN DOOR POLICY, BY INVITATION ONLY.

97.

'Bottom-up' is not more workshops but at the bottom of the organization. Changing the geography of top-down does not make it bottom up.

Leadership is not a permanent Q&A session. Systems that reinforce that ('ask the CEO', 'do you have questions for the leadership team?') perpetuate the parent-child relationship.

99.

Culture is the company's petri dish. Where things grow. Good or bad, it depends on what you throw in.

100.

M&A communication to all: 'we are going to create a new company with the best of each of us.' Problem is, the best of company A, plus the best of company B, may still be crap. If you build a new A+B=C, don't burden it with double inheritance.

101.

TO PREACH DE-HIERARCHICAL-ISATION IS TO PREACH DE-HUMANISATION, NOT THE OPPOSITE. WHEN YOU REFRAME HIERARCHIES AS THE PROBLEM INTO HIERARCHIES AS THE SOLUTION, THEN YOU'RE IN BUSINESS. THEY CAN FACILITATE, RESOURCE, CREATE, GIVE PERMISSION TO ACT AND BUFFER CONTINUITY AND REASSURANCE. THOSE FUNDAMENTALISTS WHO FIGHT HIERARCHY AS A PRINCIPLE TEND TO BE THE ONES WHO ARE LESS SMART AT MAKING GOOD USE OF IT.

'We are the fastest at customer service; we are the fastest at saying no' (Ryanair's boss Michael O'Leary). 'Here we put people first. They are the first to go' (Me, after learning from the Ryanair School of Thought).

103.

What people think and what people say are occasionally connected. Being aware of this may be lifesaving.

104.

'When the sea was calm, all ships alike; they show mastership in floating' (Shakespeare's, Coriolanus). I always thought we had too many MBAs around (including me). But what we probably have in our organizations is too many MIFs (Masters in Floating). Some are even promoted to high office. MIFs can't drive a speed boat.

105.

Busy-ness is a semi-permanent state of continuous occupation that usually carries a high degree of self-importance. It leads to an additional illness of measuring efficacy, efficiency and effectiveness by the number of activities. Being ecstatic by an overwhelming number of ratios and scores usually correlates with busy-ness.

106.

OVERINCLUSIVENESS PARALYSIS OCCURS AS A SIDE EFFECT OF GOOD INTENTIONS. MAKING SURE EVERYBODY 'GETS IT', AND ALL POSSIBLE CONSTITUENCIES HAVE BEEN INVITED TO THE MEETING, CREATES AN ORGANIZATION THAT IS A COLOSSAL INFORMATION RECYCLING SYSTEM. OVERINCLUSIVENESS IS ALWAYS, ALWAYS A SIGN OF BAD LEADERSHIP.

107.

4 targets to blame: (1) yourself,
(2) others around you, (3) the system,
(4) the global conditions. My take: tell me
who you blame, and I will give you
a full personality and risk assessment
in five minutes. For free.

108.

Process junkies hijack the territories of efficiency and destroy effectiveness. An organization that has heavily ritualised its processes does not have to think too much. When it's terminal, you don't have a company anymore, but an automatic machine. Good for cookies and sausages, mind you.

109.

Two presentation annoyances.
I hope you can see the slide from the back: always a very high probability that you can't. Can you hear me ok? Did you not bloody check before?

110.

From the tsunami of noise that Twitter is, I found a gem in one of the profiles of somebody who started to follow me: 'You can impress me with complete sentences.' I love it! Entire management development programmes could be based on this gem.

111.

WORDS ARE FINGERS
POINTING TO THE MOON.
IF YOU FOCUS TOO MUCH
ON THE FINGERS, YOU WILL
NEVER SEE THE MOON
(ZEN WISDOM). THAT IS
WHY WE NEVER SEE THE
MOON IN ORGANIZATIONS.
TOO MANY FINGERS.
TOO MANY WORDS. TOO
MANY POWERPOINTS.
TOO MANY AVATARS.

112.

I RECENTLY FOUND THE MOST HILARIOUS AND POWERFUL CURSE, APPARENTLY YIDDISH: 'MAY ALL YOUR TEETH FALL OUT EXCEPT THE ONE THAT GIVES YOU PAIN'. IT IS SERIOUSLY TEMPTING.

113.

If you want to run a successful company, you need to have at least these four values: Respect, Integrity, Communication and Excellence. Enron did.

114.

An audience is not a community. Most communication systems create audiences. Community means two-way engagement. If you aim at community but measure the effect by the size of the audience, you are measuring the volume of the bottle in centimetres.

115.

In any organization there are noise-amplifying people and noise-cancelling people. Always try to turn the volume down and go straight to the source to find out about anything, particularly rumours.

116.

In a completely self-managed organization (if you ever see one) there are no bosses. But everybody is a competitor. You trade one problem for another. It is madness and does not work. But you can easily write a book about it.

117.

TAO PHILOSOPHY FOR MANAGEMENT: 'TO KNOW WHAT ONE DOES NOT KNOW IS BEST.' NOT TO KNOW BUT BELIEVE THAT ONE DOES KNOW IS A DISEASE. ALSO, THOSE WHO KNOW DO NOT TALK ABOUT IT; THOSE WHO TALK ABOUT IT DO NOT KNOW'. AN ENTIRE LEADERSHIP PROGRAMME COULD BE CONSTRUCTED ON THESE PRINCIPLES.

118.

Large scale interventions are not small-scale ones repeated several times. The laws of scale and big numbers have nothing to do with the laws of small-scale interventions. Only exponential (multiplication) is truly large scale. Adding bodies (more people in workshops) is never scalable. Coaching, team development, individual leadership development, are not scalable. You can't coach the entire organization on, say, cultural change. That does not make them bad or useless, but certainly they are incompetent in large scale terms. Since we probably spend a good 80% of our time and efforts on small-scale repetitions, we never grasp how to tap into the entire organization. Traditional management thinking does not understand scale.

119.

Management team composition should be 'by invitation', not by a given geographical position in the organizational chart. A direct reporting line should never have an automatic position in the management team. Don't work on 'accidental management team mode', that is, you get the people the organizational chart says, not you. Invite some aliens. Disinvite some direct reports.

120.

In a regatta (I am told) you win by making less mistakes than the boat that was going to win. In business you grow by making progressively less mistakes than your competitors. Buffett says this of making money in general.

121.

We talk a lot about people needing to feel that the values of their company are consistent with their personal values. I have always found more people who are able to spot the inconsistency, the disconnect, than those who are able to articulate what their personal values are. We know what we don't like, much more than what we do like.

122.

Scientism is taking over management, so anything that can be expressed in scores and numbers is glorified regardless of the solidity of the origin. Those living under a Benign Dictatorship of Metrics can measure anything, so garbage gets duly measured and saved in pie charts.

123.

MY SOLUTION TO A 'CHICKEN AND EGG' PROBLEM IS THE OMELETTE. DEADLY SERIOUS ABOUT THIS.

124.

There is a particular form of leadership that I really dislike. It's the one in which the audio and the video don't match. What the leader says and what the leader does are not in sync, like those movies in which the lip movements don't match the audio.

"

125.

If you were to discard all management practices and principles but could keep just one, this is it: fix accountabilities, the rest is commentary.

126.

Machines work on feedback.
Minds work on feed-forward:
how we are doing against
human possibility. Feedback
is overrated.

127.

Change is social, doing it together, a praxis.
More Confucius and Tao than Aristotle. More
Roman than Greek. Individual change happens
by 'doing it in a group' and experiencing it. It's
not conceptual. It's not simply contractual either:
lose 5 kilos in 3 months. It's 'collapsing the
distinction between knowing and doing'.

Autoimmune disease is when
'the body produces antibodies that
attack its own tissue, leading to
the deterioration and sometimes
the destruction of such tissue'.
Organizations have a similar
disease. Self-inflicted problems
such as increasing complexity and
ever-increasing decision-making
processes. Give people on-the-spot
permission to solve anything. Get
3 people, not 30, to make a decision
in 3 days, not 30 days. Suppress the
immune system with a high dose
of common sense. In fact, listing
self-inflicted problems is not that
hard for any savvy manager.

STOP COMPLAINING ABOUT SILOS BETWEEN DIVISIONS. COMPUTER SCREENS ARE THE NEW SILOS. IF YOU AMALGAMATE NON-COLLABORATING SILO A WITH NON-COLLABORATING SILO B WITH THE HOPE OF CREATING A COLLABORATING NON-SILO C, GOOD LUCK. PEOPLE WILL BRING THEIR SCREENS WITH THEM ANYWAY.

130.

I have seen many corporate functions in large organizations that live in a bubble. Half Border Control police, half Bermuda Triangle of ideas, they excel at fooling many about their expertise, whilst blocking progress by creating top down, self-serving 'programmes', all competing for airtime. Nobody who has not had a frontline or operational role should ever be allowed to do those jobs, HR, OD, L&D, Comms. That includes Cambridge or Harvard graduates. In fact, especially Cambridge and Harvard graduates. The exceptions (and I have been lucky to work with some) are, well, exceptional.

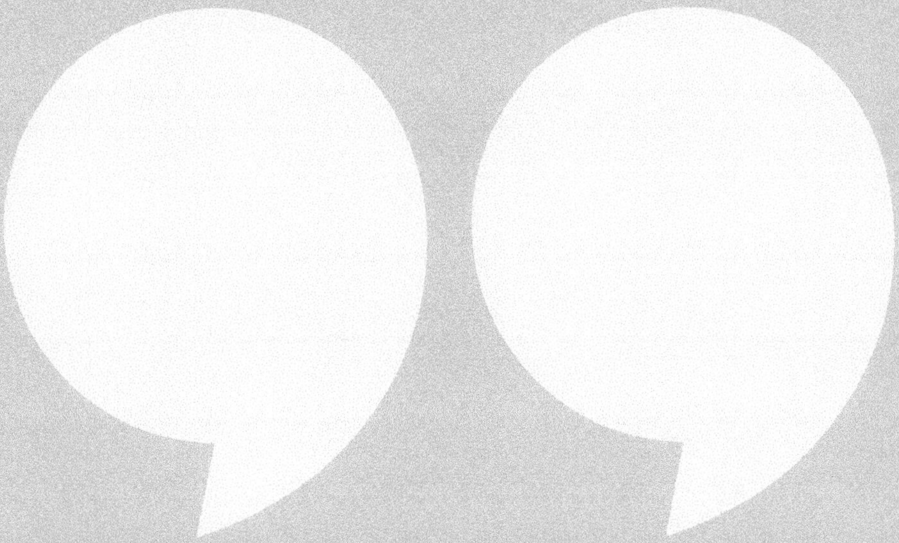

131.

Find gracious, generous people of character who want to make a difference. Let them have hope, confidence and strength. Be honest from day one: it won't be plain sailing. Give them a big common goal and ask them for help. Invite them to join you. A journey you (must) have already started. Give them the space to work in peer-to-peer mode. Treat them for who they are, not their title or their rank. Provide resources. Trust them. That night you'll sleep well. You will have started a management revolution.

132.

'STUDIES SHOW' THAT
ORGANIZATIONS WHICH
OUTPERFORM HAVE 5 STRONG
VALUES: A CLEAR SENSE OF
MISSION, A HIGH EMPOWERMENT
OF EMPLOYEES, A SOLID FOCUS
ON PERFORMANCE, A DIVERSE
WORKFORCE AND A LONG-TERM
VIEW. WHAT 'STUDIES' NEVER TELL
US IS WHY OTHER ORGANIZATIONS
WITH EXACTLY THE SAME
CHARACTERISTICS FAIL MISERABLY.
BY THE WAY, THE GROCERS ON
THE CORNER OF MY STREET FULFILS
THE 5 CRITERIA AND IS CLOSING
DOWN. HOW COME?

133.

To use a 'fixing mode' to change or to shape an organizational culture, is a bad idea. Fixing problems may be attractive to some but will always be limited in scope. Address culture as 'building'. Building something new, or better, or future proof. That may include fixing and addressing deficiencies but will attract better minds and hearts. Fixing deficiencies has never built a solid culture. Six Sigma never built one. I suspect Agile is the same.

134.

Jeff Bezos' contributions to management thinking: (1) Team size equal to how many people you can feed with a pizza; (2) Key question: will I regret not doing that?; (3) 'This is the first day of the company', repeated every year to investors. Jack Welch's (ex GE and almost management saint) contributions to management thinking: (1) workouts (glorified, relabelled traditional management practices in a box); (2) 'Forced ranking', loved by followers and HR departments, which is getting rid of the bottom 10% of performers every year (no matter who they are); (3) Contingency leadership, or the cult of 'it depends'. Bezos wins for me. By a big distance.

135.

I profoundly dislike *nombrilisme* (navel-gazing, self-absorption, ombliguismo in Spanish; the French *nombrilisme* always sounded better to me). Organizations in *nombrilisme* mode are always looking inwards, converting team reflection into Group Psychotherapy; obsessed with people development [usually run by people, who think they are developed enough to know how to develop others], worshipping 'feedback' and, in general, giving kindergartens a bad name. No wonder they do not progress fast. They spend their time on self-assessment, in permanent adolescence (*Are we friends? Just friends?*). As in Henry James's 'their relationship consisted in deciding if it existed'. Can we please move on? We will never catch that train.

136.

The best employee engagement programme is the one that doesn't exist because it is not needed. To design an employee engagement programme, think of what the organization that doesn't need one looks like. Then shape that programme. If you can.

137.

The entire Management theory and traditional MBA 'research' on management and leadership, in all its reams of paper and digital repositories, Harvard or not, including entrenched views about change and culture, all of that, contains the largest amount of bullshit ever seen in modern intellectual activity. If we were to apply the same rigour to other fields, bridges would fall down, airplanes would not fly, cars would crash, and your IT systems would not work most of the time.

138.

'Meetings' and 'teams'
are two different things.
Team equals meeting,
is a cancer. Our language
has been perverted.
'Let's bring this to the
team' usually means let's
put it on the agenda of
the next meeting. But,
the best team is the one
that never meets. Does
not need to meet. It's a
24/7 affair. For a true
team, meetings are an
add-on, not the essence.
Tip: team, as a noun,
is a structure. Forget
managing nouns. Manage
their verbs. Translation:
we need teaming up,
not more teams.

The Employee Engagement industry has managed to reinforce a mechanistic worldview of the individual in which the language of inputs and outputs dominates. Here, Employee Engagement is only good or important as long as it results in more productive employees. 'Happy cows produce better milk' is a book title in this area. Seriously. Good luck with it. It will never satisfy everybody. Question: what if engaging employees were simply morally right? Oh dear, I am smoking that again.

140.

The fundamental goal of the leader is to create 'agency', that is, the ability of people to think and act for themselves with confidence and accountability. In this respect, leadership and education are brothers. Entire politically disenfranchised groups have lost their 'agency'. The sense of lack of control is a social disaster. On a small scale, it is no different within the company.

"

Digital Transformation is a label used by many people who could not even attempt to give you a definition. It seems to include anything from Artificial Intelligence and robots, to websites for customers and faster fixing of my laptop at home. Years from now, nobody will use the term, in the same way as today, nobody refers to electricity as something that powers things.

"

142.

Work on fixed term teams. New teams need to have a 'sell by date' label and a warning: this team will disband by (date) no matter what.

143.

The word obvious has its roots in 'standing in the way'. So, 'it's obvious' may simply prevent you from moving forward.

144.

Value systems 'on the wall' are tired. They need at least some sort of desperate articulation. It's not that difficult. For example, change honesty for 'We will always tell the truth'. Honesty does not exist first. Honesty is what happens when people tell the truth.

145.

PRODUCE TWO CONTRADICTORY THOUGHTS AND LET THEM FIGHT. ACCEPT THAT BOTH MAY WIN.

146.

Drucker argued that what can't be measured can't be managed. I now know why I can't manage love, God, or a sunset. Thank God these were left outside management theory.

147.

BE PRIVATE. KEEP YOUR PRIVATE WORLD SECRET. IT'S SACRED. TRANSPARENCY OF EVERYTHING AND OPENNESS TO EVERYBODY IS POLITICALLY CORRECT EXHIBITIONISM AND NARCISSISM. TO BE ABLE TO GIVE, YOU NEED TO HAVE SOME STOCK. IF ALL IS ALREADY OUT IN THE GRAND BAZAAR OF OPENNESS, YOU WON'T GIVE ANYTHING, SO YOU WON'T SERVE.

148.

'Readiness to change'
is a red herring.
Nobody is ever ready.
We are only ready when
we act. Then, we feel we
were ready for it. Readiness
is mostly a post-hoc fallacy.
A dangerous concept to
justify doing nothing yet.
Saint Augustine, my patron
saint for readiness, knew
that: 'Lord, make me
chaste – but not yet'.

149.

I spent my MBA, many moons ago, learning about the German car manufacturing industry, the unbearable Porter's Five Forces, the miracles of Saint Jack Welch in GE, and the pseudo-science of Net Present Value. My final exam was about a small family farm in Italy. I thought the examiner was having a laugh. And probably revenge of some sort, for years of intellectual self-flagellation with Big Things Case Studies.

"

150.

The best Employee Engagement Survey has only one question: Why are you still here?

151.

If you create lots of 'agile teams'
in order to create an agile culture,
you will probably get a culture that is
not too agile but has lots of agile teams.
Many so-called agile programmes are
in need of extraordinary forms
of physiotherapy.

152.

In some organizations, all things seem well packaged, matters closed, structures are the answer to all the questions (e.g. New Unit 'so people can collaborate') and the entire architecture (structures, processes, behaviours) is clear and finished. Pristine looking, no holes, no slack, no open positions, no waste. Prepare a death certificate. If you want to live, stay in beta, or as I call it, unfinished by design.

153.

An enlightened and committed top leadership team does not guarantee an enlightened and committed organization. There are mediocre organizations with reasonably good leadership teams. How come? Maybe their power is overrated. There are also great organizations run by people of limited skill at the top. How come? This cause and effect 'dissonant curiosity' is determined to skip management thinking.

154.

360-degree feedback is the great deceiver. Another self-proclaimed 'vital management practice'. It is a self-centred and inwards looking system that is supposed to provide food for people's development. But it is also often an HR sacred cow from HR departments with a lack of imagination, sold on the idea of openness and transparency, but serving as a ritual to keep HR busy. It bypasses meaningful, truthful, day-to-day, ongoing dialogues and 24/7 mutual interchanges on behalf of a pseudo-scientific process. An alibi for managers, who don't have the guts to have honest conversations. I doubt that any job description or contract includes mental nudity and exposure to friendly fire and 'objective' input from colleagues. In the best-case scenario, do it if your boss is also included in the parade. And do it quickly, there is a lot of real work to do. In reality, it is a collective Maoist system. I have only seen collateral damage, never a seriously good thing coming out of this process. Obsessive feedback cultures are cults, not healthy organizations.

155.

The flipchart
is the largest
corporate
graveyard of ideas.
Their individual
biographies are
the Lost Scrolls of
corporate memory.

"

THE BEST RESOURCE MANAGEMENT TRAINING IS NOT TAUGHT IN BUSINESS SCHOOLS: HOW TO USE AND MANAGE RESOURCES THAT YOU DON'T OWN. WE TRAIN INSTEAD FOR MANAGING YOUR OWN BUDGET, THE ONE YOU CAN CONTROL AND OWN, WHICH IS ALWAYS A TINY PROPORTION OF ALL YOUR POSSIBILITIES. THE TRICK IS HOW TO USE RESOURCES THAT ARE NOT YOURS.

157.

Non-magic question: what are the goals and objectives? Magic question: what do we want to see by? Non-magic question: what are the outcomes? Magic question: what do we want to be proud of? Non-magic question: what's the cost of doing this? Magic question: what would be the cost of not doing this?

158.

A SIMPLE FORMAT ABOUT YOUR CULTURE TO SHARE OR AGREE WITH YOUR PEOPLE. 'THESE ARE THE 3 NON-NEGOTIABLES HERE: (1) WHEN A HAPPENS, WE WILL ALWAYS DO B, NEVER C; (2) WE WILL ALWAYS DO N, NO MATTER WHAT; (3) X WILL ALWAYS BE REWARDED, NEVER Y'.

IF YOU CAN SUBSTITUTE THE LETTERS FOR REAL THINGS, YOU ARE IN PRETTY GOOD SHAPE TO ADDRESS CULTURE. IF YOU STRUGGLE, FORGET ABOUT GOING FORWARD WITH MISSIONS, VISIONS AND THE LOT.

159.

At the end of the working day, in that little reflective corner, when the fuss of the day's schedule is gone and you are looking for that bit of humanity that has survived the brainstorms, the workshops and the war–shops, these words of the Apostle Paul to the people of Ephesus, written from a prison in Rome, are good advice: 'the sunset must not find you still angry'.

160.

'SMARTPHONES ARE THE NEW TOBACCO', SAY SOME IN NORDIC COUNTRIES. YEP!

161.

Behaviours create culture, not the other way around. Change behaviours get culture. Behaviours are copied (homo imitans) and scaled up peer-to-peer. Culture is not trainable in classrooms. Everybody copies everybody but some people are more copy-able than others. It turns out that 5-10% have very high (non-hierarchical) influence. Find them, ask for help and give them support. Tell stories of success all the time. Make sure leaders do support the peer-to-peer work, but don't interfere. This is the 'what' of Viral Change™ in a box. The 'how' is what I do for a living.

162.

CHOOSE YOUR PROBLEMS BEFORE THEY CHOOSE YOU.

163.

List your competitors, then compare yourself with anybody not on that list.

164.

Giving people a voice implies that they don't have one. More accurately it should be getting our hands off their mouths so we can hear.

165.

"

We have been taught, to the extreme of an unquestionable mantra, that we should not worry (and actually, should be pretty relaxed) about the things that are not under our control. It's the 'there is nothing I can do about it' rule. Agree on the pragmatism. Agree on the avoidance of heroic but useless action. Agree on the need to focus. But the 'there is nothing I can do about it' very often comes to the table too early, too easily, too casually. Under the liberating 'there is nothing I can do about it', we dismiss lots of things that we could and should do something about. As a rule, I never buy it in the first place.

166.

"

Beware of people telling you that their work is 'evidence-based' (medics, scientists, engineers) as if the rest of us mere mortals were sorcery based, or we just make things up. Those in defence of their 'evidence-based' worldview are often the ones more ready to make decisions on anything but evidence. Most of what passes for evidence-based is only a temporary viewpoint. In management thinking it is also a temporary viewpoint but with the additional solidity of a cream cake.

167.

Benchmarking is a race against somebody who has already won.

168.

The most important management question is 'what is the question?'. This question could be anything from disruptive to irritating. But, also liberating, since we are prone to produce answers assuming that everybody works on the same question. No decision-making meeting should start, without asking 'what is the question we have to address?'.

169.

The only way to address differences between us, is to find the common and shared spaces and then work from that territory first. Surprises may come up and differences may blur a little bit. Without the shared spaces, it will always be a shouting game.

170.

I must have an on-off switch on trust in my brain. It's never in between. For me trust is like pregnancy, it can never be 'just a little bit of'.

If you have a choice to (re) design an organization on the basis of 'who needs to do what' or 'who needs to know what', always start with 'who needs to know what'. Then, match against the alternative design based on the former 'who needs to do what'. If there is no good match, you have just discovered a problem and saved thousands on consulting fees to rescue an unworkable organizational structure.

172.

The following qualify for early retirement on compassionate grounds due to their poor health, in some cases terminal illness: Agile, neuro-anything (as in neuro-leadership and neuro-marketing), employee engagement surveys, annual performance management systems, 360 feedback, working from home (as a sign of how flexible we are), talking about VUCA, Change Management à la Kotter, gender targets (as a sign of how diverse we are), mindset-change programmes (I have worked as a clinical psychiatrist for 15 years of my life and I have never seen a mindset, no idea what they look like; but I've seen lots of behaviours, I know what to do with those) and purpose. Purpose is really, really exhausted and has asked for a career break, but I don't know whether it will ever be back. It has been occupying the old Mission and Vision discredited spaces and has become so overworked that it has grown grey hair. It also has nasty arthritis.

173.

'A MAN WITHOUT A SMILE CAN'T OPEN A SHOP', THE CHINESE PROVERB SAYS. APPLY AD LIBITUM IN ORGANIZATIONS, NO RESTRICTIONS, IT HAS NOTHING TO DO WITH SHOPS.

174.

The current shelf life of a Best Practice is 5 minutes, and it's been a while since I last checked.

175.

THE 'SORRY-I-HAVE-TO-GO-TO-ANOTHER MEETING' PEOPLE SHOULD ALWAYS BE ENCOURAGED TO GO STRAIGHT TO THAT ONE AND BYPASS YOURS.

176.

We want the organizational flexibility of Lego. We recruit for the rigidity of a jigsaw: pieces that fit perfectly in a space. When a jigsaw piece goes on maternity leave, or leaves the company, we will replace it with a similar piece that needs to fit in. Exactly. No replacement, hole is visible, jigsaw incomplete. The jigsaw gives us the comfort of the permanent structure of a castle (looks like a castle, the picture of a castle is on the box, not a dragon, or a boat, it's that particular castle) but tomorrow we want the castle to be a gazelle, or maybe Formula 1, or perhaps something googlesque. The jigsaw needs the 'expert pieces', the Lego needs the re-usable pieces. The jigsaw is fixed, no dragons with the pieces of a boat. The Lego is a reconfigurable, dragon today, farmhouse tomorrow. Lego or jigsaw, this is all you need to decide in organizational design. Organizational charts are the picture of jigsaws.

177.

Try this. In this meeting, any
statement related to an answer,
or a position after brainstorming,
or at the time of making a decision,
must not start with 'it depends'.
Write this rule on a flipchart.
'It depends' is banned. These
things will happen: (1) people will
struggle a lot, (2) people will laugh
a lot, (3) people will find creative
ways to circumvent the prohibition,
(4) at the very least, you'll make the
point that the permanent 'sitting on
the fence status' ('it depends') that
characterises many team dynamics
will not be acceptable this time.

178.

WE OFTEN LACK THE DISCIPLINE OF
QUESTIONING. PERHAPS WE LOST IT IN
KINDERGARTEN. BUT, GOOD NEWS, WE CAN
BUILD IT BACK BY PRACTISING. IT'S LIKE
GOING TO THE GYM, BUT IN YOUR HEAD.
AND PREPAID LIFE MEMBERSHIP.

179.

Non magic: what is the latest intelligence
and new data? Magic: what's the story?
Non magic: give me feedback from the
strategy meeting today. Magic: so, what's the
story? Non magic: mum, could you explain
to me again how the dragon leveraged his
competitive advantage to get to the princess?
(don't worry, it's not going to happen).

180.

PEER POWER: IF MANAGERS SAY, 'SAFETY IS FIRST', THE IMPACT MAY BE RELATIVE. THE DICTATION IS TOTALLY EXPECTED. THIS IS WHAT THEY ARE SUPPOSED TO SAY. IF MY PEER SAYS, 'SAFETY IS FIRST', I'M BEGINNING TO PAY ATTENTION. IT'S NOT EXPECTED, WE WERE TALKING FOOTBALL AND HOLIDAYS. (WHAT IS THE MATTER WITH HIM?) BUT I HEAR IT. TELL ME MORE. PEER-TO-PEER IS STRONGER THAN MANAGERIAL TOP DOWN.

181.

My kind of people are those who, in front of a crap and lousy process, make things happen first and then find the energy to tackle the crap process and change it. Not the other way around. Those who need to fix processes and procedures first for them to be able to act, are themselves high maintenance. Put them together and nothing will ever get done.

182.

SOME ORGANIZATIONS SHOULD HAVE A BIG SIGN AT THE FRONT DOOR QUOTING DANTE'S INFERNO: 'ABANDON ALL HOPE WHEN ENTERING HERE'.

WHY ON EARTH DO SOME PEOPLE START THEIR CVS WITH 'I AM A THOUGHT LEADER' OR 'I AM AN INFLUENCER'? SERIOUSLY.

184.

The only skill needed in a dialogue is not to hear what the other says but to interpret it: what is behind his question? What's underneath it? What is the unsaid?

185.

The industry of Employee Engagement (and there is a big one) says that companies with high employee engagement (as measured by some kind of artificial tool) are more successful. And produces 'studies' to prove it. Employee engagement is clearly portrayed as the reason for success, so the path is clear: how can we get more of it? My view is that success creates employee engagement, not the other way around. If you want high employee engagement, run a successful organization. I know it's rather inconvenient to think this way.

186.

I have met a big boss who wrote memos, long hand, for his secretary to type and send by normal mail. Another one who had his secretary printing his emails and sending them by FedEx to him. A client who did not know the password for his computer since he had never 'been' in the corner of his large office, where the never-used computer screen lived. Another who played golf in his office and moved the furniture around each time. Another who gave her direct report clear advice for her team: let them fail. Who needs field experience with Amazonian tribes to gain an anthropological degree, when all the surviving exotics are on the payroll?

187.

I've met many top leaders in my life whose greatest merit seemed to be avoiding mistakes, by letting others make them for them. They climbed to the top on grounds of stainless purity and immaculate protection of themselves. They survived reorganizations one after another, with Darwinian perfection until the point at which the severance package was not to be refused anymore. They called this point 'time to move on'. But having been motionless all their life, they could only end up being advisers or armchair investors or Board non execs. At this point they are incredibly skilful at pronouncing platitudes and they continue their working life with the same total lack of 'skin in the game' that has been their key feature until then.

188.

Victimism (adopting a victim role) is one of the most powerful toxic conditions that any organization can have within it. The two versions, individual victimism and collective victimism, are equally intoxicating. Hijacking the territory of true victims, these corporate squatters tend to gain attention, sympathy and easy membership of Unions. Once the space is taken, the behaviours can be easily reinforced by the smallest of grievances and the natural sympathy to victims from anybody. It's a perfect space for entitlement and lack of accountability. Collective victimism (of an organization, a group, a division, a team) is a problem which will never be resolved by rational confrontation, since the survival of these pseudo-victims depends on never leaving their role completely. In the same way that nations need enemies to protect their identity, corporate victimism needs a constant degree of unfairness and injustice to not have to leave the territory.

189.

I WISH I COULD RESPECT
PEOPLE NOT IN A HURRY
BUT, UNFORTUNATELY,
I NEVER SEEM TO MANAGE
TO MEET THEM.

190.

When the physicist Wolfgang Pauli was shown a paper by a young colleague, he described it as 'not even wrong'. The 'not even wrong' category is perhaps the most devastating qualification one can get since that historical point. Pauli was famous for his critical thinking. He once replied to the soviet physicist Lev Landau with 'What you said was so confused that one could not tell whether it was nonsense or not'. I wonder what the Paulinian treatment would be of the Management Theory and the Top Business School's intellectual approach to reality? I would not want to know. Not even, what?

191.

A top leadership team should not be composed of people, who are representing their functions or business units in the company, reporting to the boss. For example, I represent R&D, you represent France, she represents Finance, he represents Commercial, etc. It's an ambassadorial model. A true top leadership team is the one in which the members of that team represent in the opposite direction: the company in their functions and business units. I represent the company in R&D, you represent the company in France, her, the company in the Finance Division, that colleague represents the company in the Commercial organization, etc. Management thinking has got the arrow of the vector in the wrong direction. The arrow should not look up, but down.

192.

Social media is a colossal echo chamber where all cognitive processes are surrendered to one single driver: confirmation bias. People read what they want to read. People hear what they want to hear. Preconceived ideas are confirmed. Common enemies become more common. The system increases mistrust of others outside the chamber, whilst reinforcing one single acceptable worldview. Homophily (bonding and binding with 'people like me') rises steeply. The population in that colossal echo chamber becomes more homogeneous and predictable all the time, so that social media algorithms become more robust and your targeted news and advertising reaches you safely and securely. It's a wonderful life.

193.

A world class movement in Health Care is trying to switch the emphasis from 'what is the matter?' (your pain, symptoms, difficulties) to 'what matters to you?'. For a patient, 'the matter' may be the difficulty in breathing that gets him hospitalised. 'What matters to him', may be, not being able to attend his niece's wedding. An entire compassionate, human culture can be built on the premise of asking the question 'what matters to you?' Our world of management and organizations could learn a thing or two from this.

194.

The Saint Francis School of Management is at the top of my personal ranking. It was created in the 13th Century in Assisi, Italy, and had one single amalgamated course on communications, change, leadership and organizational development. The course was very short. In fact, the training book contained one single page with a single sentence: 'Preach the Gospel all the time; when necessary use words.' An entire worldview, an entire lifestyle, an entire leadership system, from this 'use words when necessary'.

We have an obsession with the homogeneous organizational model and an aversion to combining different models under one roof. This flawed homogeneity, in which all divisions or groups need to look the same, feel the same, smell the same, report the same way and drink from the same communications water, will never be ahead of the game. Borrowing from, and paraphrasing, Nassim Taleb in another context, it should be possible to be presidential at top leadership level, movie maker (together for a while, then disband) at group or division level, and, for example, communist at team level. Big Consulting and gurus preach Model A vs Model C, Model X versus Model Y. That worries me. What we need is the art of cohabitation of Model A and B and X and Y under the same roof. Good leadership is good hosting.

196.

When organizations grow, their systems
and processes grow. When organizations
grow, they are better able to address
their complex, external environment.
To react to that complex environment,
the organization's internal systems
and processes become more complex.
At some point, managing the internal
complexity becomes a greater problem
than managing the complexity of the
environment. The airtime becomes
internally consumed. The word customer
is suddenly an inwards looking concept.
The new, more complex internal systems
attract even more internal complexity.
The escalation is fast. 10 guys is a start-up.
At 20, an entire HR department comes
from nowhere. At 200, a new internal
enterprise digital customer blah blah
blah system is bought. From here on,
the possibilities are endless.

197.

Revere the past, then move forward and leave it to the archaeologists.

198.

Culture is the difference between 30 people making a decision in 30 days, or 3 people making the same decision in 3 days. Culture is the difference between hiring costly employees and retaining them, or hiring costly employees and losing them after 6 months. Culture is the difference between making a decision and implementing it, or making the same decision and waiting to see if it sticks or people take it seriously. Culture is the difference between agreeing the plan in the meeting room, or trashing it at the break in the toilets. Culture is hard stuff. Do you need me to give you an ROI on these differences?

199.

People with all the answers are overqualified for any job.

200.

Cultures are not created by training. If you need new ethics in your system, because you've got some problems with dodgy behaviour, you don't solve it by sending all managers on a course about Ethics at a business school (as investment banks and financial institutions have done several times). Enron did not need more training in Ethics. BP, post Deepwater, did not need more training in Safety. Training is rarely the solution most of the time.

The Second Flipping Book

1. **People's loyalty is to the tribe first (function, team, product, brand), then to the larger vision.** That is why many corporate, top-down communication programmes that send the same message to everybody, without tribal distinction, are so inefficient. In pharma, I've seen R&D chemists in love with some chemical processes leading to a beautiful shortcut to a new potential drug, who are more in love with the enzyme than with treating patients. Does it make them bad human beings?

2. **Value systems 'on the wall' are more likely to denote a scarcity of them than a serious aspiration.** This rule of thumb has always served me well and is very much alive today. It annoys many people, so keep it secret. Promise me?

3. **Peer-to-peer networks are dynamite. Teams are ground transportation, not Formula 1.** We still live in what I call *teamocracies. Teamocracies* are responsible for a great deal of the slowness of the place and its dismal innovation.

4. **'The system will prevent itself from solving the problems it creates'.** Read *'The Systems Bible: The Beginner's Guide to Systems Large and Small'* (2003) by John Gall. A wealth of suggestions without having to attend a course on Systems and Complexity Theory at the Santa Fe Institute.

5. **Skin in the game.** Read Nassim Taleb's *'Skin in the game'* (2019). His writing does not touch 'management' as much as other areas such as politics, risk, or societal issues. He is probably one of the best minds in the West. Also, an unforgiving critic of what he calls IYIs (intellectual, yet idiots). Never pick a fight with Taleb on Twitter. Or anywhere.

6. **Trust, engagement and happiness are outcomes.** This confusion between inputs and outputs in the organization has claimed many fiascos but has made many consultants rich as well. Talking about what must go in, planning for and measuring those inputs is much easier. That is why we glorify 'putting effort' into something. The education system in England measures effort. I can understand the good intentions, but it diverts a lot of attention to the input. Teachers tend to like that.

7. **To complain about a lack of diversity and inclusion you have to already be reasonably diverse and inclusive.** Read *'The Rise of Victimhood Culture: Microaggressions, Safe Spaces, and the New Culture Wars'* (2018), by Bradley Campbell and Jason Manning. We are all going mad in socio-political correctness, not only in US colleges but in organizations too.

8. **There is only one strategy test: what will you tell the children?** My children, your children, their children, the children. Apply wisely and broadly. Once you look them in the eyes, you'll know straight away if the grandiose strategy you are proclaiming has any legs. What we will tell the children is 'the red face test' of leadership.

9. **'Act as if you were an owner'.** I don't know who created this absurdity but, congrats, it did very well in the management magical thinking weaponry.

10. **People who ask 'what is in it for me' should never be given an answer.** People always get a bit shocked when I push for this. I am ruthless with this rule. But I suggest a benign alternative answer: 'I can't speak for you, but for me...'

11. **There are people with whom you share a problem and you always end up with two.** Or maybe three. The question is not whether but when you'll find them. Their disposition to 'listening' and 'understanding' often correlates with their ability to amplify the problem.

12. **The greatest liability of people 'who have done this before'.** One of my best accomplishments as a consultant was to (successfully) recommend as head of pharma R&D somebody who had never worked in drug development. He had tons of highly embarrassing and disruptive questions. He was brilliant at his job.

13. **Charismatic leadership.** It's fashionable to say that this is an old concept. In my old days as a medical student, we used to complain about what were called, 'magisterial lectures'. When

we didn't have good 'magisters', they were awful indeed. When they were good, the auditorium was always full.

14. **Companies that have become proficient at solving problems, tend to create more problems (to be solved).** *Solutionism* is a disease. Amen.

15. **People often say, organizations have a big communication problem.** It's a disturbing thought, but we overcommunicate. We have been told 'communicate, communicate, communicate, never cease to communicate'. Which is, in itself, a form of overcommunication. We overcommunicate because we lack imagination and putting things on fancy PowerPoints comes in very handy. If we communicated less, we might even get more attention.

16. **You are your calendar. Don't tell me your title, show me your Outlook calendar.** In fact, I have asked to see calendars many times. Similarly, if you run a Word Cloud on a pile of corporate documents (or script in the website) you can get a pretty accurate picture of the culture.

17. **Entire company culture efforts have been hijacked by numbers in a score system.** There is a whole industry of Employee Engagement cum survey that has proven very resilient despite its obvious flaws. If I had a pound/euro/dollar for every (private) hypercritic in an organization who is actually in charge of implementing this stuff, I could go on a Sabbatical.

18. **Leaders with solid values don't go around saying 'these are my solid values'.** This rule of mine has survived time. It's incredibly robust. It's also cheap to use it. You'll spot the characters straight away. Zero cost.

19. **Top leadership role modelling is overrated.** Read my book *Homo Imitans* (2011). Also, read the Edelman Trust Barometer which Mr Google will be happy to show you.

20. **The ultimate role of the leader is to lose control.** I launched this in my book *Disruptive Ideas* in 2008. Losing control is the ultimate way to gain it. There are 29 other disruptive ideas there, as well as the basis for my Disruptive Ideas seminar.

21. **The best question is the one that has no answer.** Maybe our education system educates for answering and not for questioning. Our organizations are simply the fruit of the education of its people. 'Teach to the test' gets robots.

22. **If you have a lot of analytical people who can dissect an elephant and have become proficient in anything to do with its parts.** The tale of the blind men and the elephant is very old, probably of Indian origin. Each blind person thinks the 'elephant' is only the part they can touch. I explore this in my book *'New Leaders Wanted'* (2015)

23. **Business Case Studies are a bad form of investigative journalism.** The Case Study Industry is a big one, and with lots of money and interests involved. Can't think of a greater culprit in the progressive irrelevance of Business Schools than the pervasive obsession with Case Studies.

24. **Finance is soft, culture is hard.** The hard-soft, binary view of competences has done more damage than good. When people talk about the soft skills of leadership, I personally think spreadsheets.

25. **Passion is overrated. Most of the time, it is hard work.** I have made myself terribly unpopular with this. There is a corporate version of 'All we need is love' which is 'All we need is passion'. Usually sung by people who never had to bear the consequences of lots of passionate, single idea people, creating havoc. I definitely love passion, as a bonus, in a well-organized and aligned group. Also, *'any corpse on Everest was once a very motivated and passionate person'.* Somebody said that. Probably not a climber.

26. **I am very sorry to have to bring bad news to you: there is no 'They'.** I have seen this 'They' all over the place, including executive boards referring to an imaginary external power. The language of 'They' is pervasive, viral, toxic. Declare it banned. Even better, have a donation box to the Goddess. Any use of 'They', 10 bucks.

27. **Culture is what happens when compliance leaves the room.** There are several variations of this around. When nobody sees you, for example. It's a good way to bring attention to the invisible. The same applies to what people say (in that culture) which is often less important than what is unsaid. The unsaid is always far more revealing than the said. Far more interesting for sure.

28. **We have blindly glorified collaboration.** Collaboration does not distinguish between good guys and bad guys. The former need tools to improve it, the latter need quarantine to prevent it.

29. **Individual change does not precede social change.** It suits standard psychological views to think in sequence: mental state first, behaviour as a consequence. Courage first, action after. Readiness first, then you act. We have a machine-like approach of the mind, input this, output after. It's hard to beat the conventional wisdom and, frankly, it may be a lost battle. However, the reality is that those 'preconditions' are fictional. They are a post-hoc explanation of actions. Regardless of the intellectual war about this (for which I declare myself on strike) the fact is that the constant invocation of the pre-condition has prevented millions of people to act today (waiting for the miraculous pre-condition) and change the bit of the world they were supposed to change.

30. **All useless or ineffective processes that seem untouchable, are in fact rituals that have nothing to do with the declared goal of the process.** Rituals deserve a big place in organizational thinking. It should have been up to Corporate Anthropology to teach us, but Corporate Anthropology lost the plot a long time ago. After field work in Africa (Papua New Guinea is already done) their graduates became market research managers for Unilever.

31. **Process junkies need treatment.** There isn't a process to fall in love, or a process to appreciate Mahler's Fifth. Yes, yes, I have heard the manufacturing guys too. They need processes. Great revelation. We do too. There is also a process to get the kids to school in the morning, but normal people don't think that way.

32. **Leadership is a club to which Mandela, Hitler, Mother Teresa, Mao, Obama, Tony Soprano and Pope Francis belong. This club has the most terrible admissions policy.** Leadership (as an industry) is a colossal sales operation that produces reams of lists of 'unequivocal traits' (of leaders) to suit the buyer. Probably the best books on leadership are in the Biography section of bookshops, not in the management bazaar.

33. **Trust is nonlinear (excuse my language). Usually it's hard or long to gain, but it's always one screw up away from killing it.** How unfair!

34. **The most toxic kind of employee or manager is the Saviour.** There are lots and lots of people who want to save you. From failure, from sin, from a bad decision, from bad morals. That's often problematic enough. To have one of these as your manager, is another different dimension. One of my senior colleagues in my previous corporate life saw himself as the Saviour of all people. He used to say, 'let them fail'. I regret not having called him out at the time.

35. **To be very effective you have to be a bit inefficient.** Shadow jobs are inefficient, they consume extra resources. Overlapping job descriptions ditto. Management efficiency has taught us one person one box, no duplications, efficient use of resources. Otherwise this is a waste. Waste is bad. But some of the 'waste' is in fact the glue. Call it a certain degree of redundancy of slack in the system. I call it oxygen. To be very efficient you need to allow for the unpredictable, the extra-ordinary, the extended positive consequences. While total inefficiency will lead to disaster, some inefficiencies will fuel greater success.

36. **Corporate Social Responsibility (CSR) is tested everyday with employees in the corridor.** You may not pollute rivers but pollution lives around you. You may give to charity but be most uncharitable with your teams. You may be green to the outside, but very dark inside.

37. **Diversity and Inclusion start with diversity of ideas and opinions, and end on gender.** Many Diversity and Inclusion programmes in organizations are music to calm the popular voice. Gender parity at the top Board with terrible equity at the bottom is an embarrassment. I could not care less if 50% of the Board are women if employees are treated like robots.

38. **Don't read anything that starts with 'research has shown'.** This is a good opportunity, believe me, you can skim through and discard lots. People who know the research, or have done it, or simply know what they are talking about, will never write that 'research shows' sentence.

39. **Stop announcing change.** Many reorganizations and change programmes are loudly announced to people with the best of intentions, so people get used to the idea. There may be a legal requirement for an early warning in some countries. But going over the top on this, is simply prolonging the agony and creating extraordinary anxiety. If I sound as though I'm advocating secrecy, I will change the sound. I am advocating sanity. Very frequently I have found myself in situations when the client's announcement of change will impact on a tiny minority, yet the apocalyptic communication has created lots of sleepless nights for people who had no reason not to sleep well.

40. **Demonising hierarchy is easy and politically correct but not terribly efficient.** My very first article on management topics, after my time as a clinical psychiatrist, was entitled *'Kings or Cousins'*. Get rid of the tyranny of the king, but get the tyranny of cousins, barons and local leaders. It's a choice. Hierarchy will never go away, no matter how attractive and money making for consultants that idea may be. Fighting hierarchy is fighting our natural world, our own animal nature. Hierarchy belongs to the category of the certainty of 'Death and taxes'. The practical thing to do is to decide on the type of hierarchy, quality and quantity. The dichotomy hierarchical versus non-hierarchical organizations has been fabricated in Academia and Consulting because it's sexy, forward looking and a good topic for an article in *Harvard Business Review*.

41. **A culture of safety is not the same as a culture of training in safety.** Throwing money at training is safe. It shows commitment, gives you scores as a good employer and it is relatively easy to implement. I am not against training. Hardly. But I am against training as a solution for all seasons. I have seen incredibly well-trained sales forces delivering poor sales result and being given more training as a remedy. A culture of obsessive training creates a fantastic culture of training, not necessarily the culture of the topic people are supposed to be trained for.

42. **Create a counter-epidemic.** Most behavioural problems at scale need a social treatment. In this sense, the wisdom of 'one person at a time', 'one thing at a time' makes for good headlines but, this slow cooking approach to change only makes sense to those who have a lot of time in front of them.

43. **In any change programme (whatever that may mean) the most important thing is to know what is not for changing.** It's amazing how this is so difficult to articulate. Presumably, values, for example, are not for change. I always ask my client to start the communication on change by what is not changing.

44. **If you have two guys who think the same, fire one of them.** I am pretty sure Tom Peters said that. He said so many (good) things that the statistics quoting him are always in his favour.

45. **There are only 3 reasons why people do what they do: because they are told to, because they want to, and because others do it.** Our Viral Change™ programmes start by unapologetically using the 'because others do' (peer-to-peer) with the aim of showing real benefits that make 'people want to do'. Which will make the 'told to do' redundant. I learnt in a programme at the Aspen Institute, many moons ago, (by a fellow participant who was a CIA manager) that in the early days of Microsoft, there was a small layer at the top, perhaps less than 100, who people called 'the volunteers'. They had made so much money already that none of them needed to work anymore. It stuck with me since. And no, I did not have any other conversations with the CIA lady.

46. **Decouple influence and hierarchy.** This has been a muddle for a long time. Read the Edelman Trust Barometer for insights into influence in the organization. Visit orgmapper. com to understand how to find the real influencers in the organization. Today, 'Influencer programmes' are becoming fashionable in many companies. But it's so frustrating to see how these companies do not know exactly what to do with the pool, other than, err, ask them to influence. Through workshops on influence for influencers and having pioneered Viral Change™, I am unapologetically biased towards the organizational and cultural solution that it provides.

47. **Some organizations are in permanent rehearsal-mode.** In those, the present is always preparation, not a reality. They have an imbalance 'thinking of doing, planning for doing and saying we will be doing' to 'doing', in the order of 10:1. Even the fashionable 'future of work' talk consumes the present big time. No wonder we have glorified benchmarking. We love looking back.

48. **When the organization works as an aggregation of echo chambers.** I have never underestimated the importance of injecting fresh air in... anything. All management structures in the organization should have their 'sell by date' label, at which point, spring cleaning, opening windows and an injection of fresh air is mandatory. We can debate how drastic and how broad, but an unchallenged continuity of everything is simply lethal.

49. **'Assume goodwill' is a good start.** It may sound naïve, but it opens lots of possibilities to humanizing the place. It may be more powerful than you think.

50. **The company is not an Internal Diplomatic Service where people always act as if they are representing somebody else other than themselves.** A long time ago I described two models of teams. In the ambassadorial model, everybody is an ambassador, a well-paid avatar. In the professional services (à la Tom Peters) model, people represent themselves (Taleb's 'skin in the game'). Most of our matrix-driven *teamocracies* work on an ambassadorial model. The meeting is the grand bazaar of visitors from far away. Not much gets done there, because all is decided elsewhere. In a matrix system, the game is always elsewhere.

51. **In the first 50 days of a new CEO, he should cut corporate initiatives by half.** One of the most popular in my *Disruptive Ideas* (2008) book. Also, the one people pay more lip service to.

52. **Nasty, sceptical, negative, toxic people cannot be changed by rational appeal, performance management or special prayers.** In my previous life as a psychiatrist, many of my most successful 'interventions' were transplants. Not of organs but of the entire being to a new, different, a bit unknown (but relatively safe) territory. Temporarily (but drastically) changing the family environment, for example, at a distance, always paid off. My main question was often 'where is your most distant relative with a house and a room?'

53. **The 9 to 5 management language should match the after 5 language with kids and wives and husbands.** Our corporate language is robotic. We don't need to wait for the robots to come. They have been here for a while, unnoticed, and with a degree from Harvard.

54. **'It is difficult to get a man to understand something, when his salary depends on his not understanding it'.** This quote is from Upton Sinclair, an American writer who died in 1968. He wrote almost 100 books.

55. **Culture is more of a landscape and a tapestry than excel spreadsheets and bar charts.** OK, I got a bit poetic here, but if you think tapestry, you have a much better chance to understand culture than those PowerPoints from Big Consulting.

56. **Town Hall meetings are fireworks. Offsite meetings are corporate flash mobs.** They both belong to the tyranny of the one-off, something we are masters of in organizations. They are part of what I call 'World I' in my book *Homo Imitans* (2011) and which is also at the core of Viral Change™, that is, the distinction between World I (Communications) and World II (behavioural).

57. **Change Management is dead. It needs a funeral not a function.** The term has become so overused that it is meaningless. Change management often stands for 'making stuff happen'. IT people hijacked it a long time ago and it means implementation. Managers of change use it and it often means 8 meaningless steps that cannot be implemented sequentially in real life. Technology implementation people use it but it means anything that is not the technology side. With such levels of accuracy, I prefer not to treat my house move as change management. Or, I will never move, or it will cost me 10 times more, or the expensive Russian porcelain will be broken.

58. **Total self-management.** There is a cult view of self-management that portrays it as the Holy Grail. I am afraid, it's not Grail and there's nothing Holy about it. There are very few exceptions of that working but hundreds of failures. Of course, when failed, people would say 'it had not been implemented properly'. Which is what was said of communism. 'Pockets of self-management', yes. It's a very different story from 'total self-management'.

59. **Why can highly paid Supremoes of Management not process more than 3 bottom liners and 3 bullet points?** There is little doubt that humanity is losing cognitive power. Attention span is now closer to that of the goldfish, said to be 5 seconds. There is magical thinking about 'the good number of'. 3 seems to be accepted, 5 is stretching it and 10 clearly overwhelming. Seriously?

60. **I call 'impossible to disagree with'**, any plans or proposals that do not trigger some level of discomfort. They are to be treated as suspicious. Valium-like statements of intentions are always well received by people who want an easy life, or decaffeinated coffee. When 'impossible to disagree with' is the climax of the qualification, you have been sedated.

61. **Surveys tell you the what, almost never the why. Maybe this is why they are so popular.** I have this rule of thumb: For every formal survey of, say, 100 people, I want people to personally interview at least 50. Surveys lead us to Big Data. Anthropology to Small Data. Big Data without the Small Data (at least in the human capital business) misses lots of critical 'whys'. I am not anti-surveys but most certainly I am anti-surveys only.

62. **'The Stone Age did not end because we ran out of stones; it ended because we invented new tools'.** Attributed to a former Saudi Oil Minister. I read it in the New York Times, so it must be right.

63. ***Teamocracy* has dominated organizational life.** Teams, as people usually understand them, are not the ultimate form of collaboration. Riding the network is far more important than inhabiting a team. Read *New Leaders Wanted* (2017).

64. **Established management thinking is an intellectual collage: Starbucks did that, HSBC did that, Best Buy did that.** *'Give me an example'* people say. Sure, no problem, the dark side or the light side of the same company? *'Just give it to me, for goodness sake'.*

65. **Success, it's never the opposite of failure. Failure is never the opposite of success.** Learnt from my praxis. When I divide a leadership team into two groups, one to write the script of how they will have succeeded in one year, and the other to write the script on how they will have failed one year later, I never get complete mirror outputs. And the ones on failure always finish much earlier in the exercise.

66. **I can only work with people who (1) don't take themselves too seriously, (2) can use full sentences, (3) don't do 'small difference', (4) have unlimited curiosity and, (5) they are faster than me.** Ok, I am aware my possibilities shrink enormously.

67. **Smoking kills, don't drink and drive, get the flu vaccination, wear the safety gear, etc.** Most traditional change management models are based on the assumed power of communication. The failure rate is embarrassing. Non-smoking depends largely on how many people around you don't smoke. Even if banned in places. The vaccination rate depends largely on how many other people you know have done it. Ditto for drinking and driving, and for safety. 'Social' has the power. Rational understanding is almost powerless.

68. **Innovation has to do with seeking unpredictable answers.** Also, we plan for predictable and repetitive processes for good reasons. But these reasons never work when looking for innovation. Innovation and replicable processes are the Capulet and the Montague of management. There is no 'it's both'. Romeo always dies.

69. **A reason why it's so difficult to shape culture in the areas of Safety or Ethics & Good Conduct. Reward safety, not avoidance of the unsafe.** In behavioural terms, the focus has to be on the positive and its enhancement or multiplication. The focus on the positive is often seen as Pollyanna management and therefore dismissed. Please don't quote me. The alpha-male and alpha-female manager secretly love the negative, the problem, the error, the fiasco, the crisis, the issue, the fixing needs. The behavioural glasses force you to look for the opposite so it can be reinforced. This real behavioural approach almost always loses.

70. **Bermuda Triangles in the company: flip charts, intranets, training binders, etc.** At home, it's my washing machine: give it socks, they will never come back, or in the best case they go in as married and come back as single, a traumatic diving experience of some sort, I guess.

71. **Many long, complex and expensive reorganization projects led by Big Consulting Groups make companies fully prepared for their past.** Fully prepared to win the last war. They create adaptation (so it's late) or increase flexibility (so that they can be hit again), but never an antifragile company 'that which grows from disorder'. Read Taleb's *Antifragile* (2013). Read it twice. I read it once a year.

72. **Employees should treat their bosses as their investment fund managers.** People should behave like investors of their own human capital. The place of work will be a place of growth, or it's not worth it. Nobody willingly invests to find himself in the negative, or with no growth, at the end of the year. If people cannot have their personal market value increased at the end of the year, I would question the wisdom of being there. I would change my investment fund manager (employer). Ditto for consultants and their clients. The 'investors metaphor' is from Thomas O. Davenport, as far back as 1999.

73. **The cost of not doing something is one of the most forgotten questions in management.** This is a standard question in our leadership, design and Viral Change™ practices.

74. **'I am unconditionally supportive and fully behind the project, but I have 3 concerns.'** From a recent very supportive client.

75. **Habits have no meaning, they create it. Start with behaviours, get meaning.** With my behavioural hat on, meaning comes after I do meaningful things. This hat is annoying to many, I know, because we think the other way around. Do religious believers believe first and then perform rituals according to their beliefs? Would it be entirely possible that people who perform some rituals end up believing? It's a flipping question. Any quick dismissal of the latter, just because it does not fit our thinking, may be comfortable but probably unwise.

76. **We have made character, virtue or goodness uncomfortable terms in the organization.** Management sanitised itself a long time ago from humanistic contaminations. Ok, the real, confident alfa management. Bring character back! If you want something more 'modern', try David Brooks' *The Road to Character* (2016) or his latest *'The Second Mountain'* (2019). Brooks is a conservative writer and columnist in The New York Times, who most liberals read. It tends to disappoint both sides. Passionate about the 'fabric of society' he leads an initiative within The Aspen Institute called 'Weave: The Social Fabric Project'. Worth a read on their website.

77. **'A study in Harvard Business Review' and 'A new 3 star Michelin McDonald's'.** My hypercriticism may be annoying. I just can't reconcile critical thinking and some top academic publications, from which the 'Harvard Business Review' represents the Biblical reference. I don't get it.

78. **I make my best clients restless; the others are content. The very best become friends.** It's much easier to provide comfort than restlessness. It's a choice. On our website we publicise that we won't always tell people what they want to hear. If the client wants that, to hear what they want to hear, we give them the phone number of our competitors.

79. **Some leaders distinguish themselves by their imminent irrelevance, but the problem is that, unfortunately, imminence seems to prolong itself forever.** Irrelevance and longevity can easily travel together. I can confirm.

80. **If the company is overheating and has no thermostat, every day without an explosion is pure luck.** Inspired by the very readable anthropologist Thomas Hylland Eriksen. I love his book *'Small Places, Large Issues'* which has had several editions. His *'Overheating: an anthropology of Accelerated Change'* was published in 2016. If you read one single book on Anthropology, read his *'Small Places'*.

81. **Do it right the first time, but also experiment and learn from mistakes.** The 'It-is-both-school-of-thought' is highly popular. Almost as popular as the 'It-depends-school-of-thought'. The 'it's both' argument is as cheap as it is predictable and welcomed by people. When 'it's both', you don't have to think anymore. That solves lots of problems.

82. **Leaders have two hats.** This 'two hats' leadership is at the core of Viral Change™. There is (1) hierarchical and top down, (2) distributed (significant number of natural leaders and people of influence with no correlation with their position in the hierarchy, and (3) backstage, based upon the need for the top down leaders to support from the back, not the front. Backstage Leadership™ is the bridge between the hierarchy and the peer-to-peer networks. Even the Intellectual Property

Office understood that when they granted us the Backstage Leadership™ Trademark. I often think that we were more successful with the IP office than with some corporate VPs.

83. **For every piece of business advice that makes sense there is an opposite that makes equal sense.** Centralise for the next 5 years, decentralise for the following 5? That would be too cynical. Yet, fortunes have been created. In the 'Three Envelopes' tale, a new CEO is left with three envelopes by the previous one, only to be opened one by one at any big crisis. At the first crisis, the first envelope is opened. It contains a card with a message: 'Centralise'. At the second crisis, the card in the second envelope reads: 'Decentralise'. At the third crisis, the card says: 'Prepare three envelopes'.

84. **Welcome to Townville. Population 350, churches 3, bars 11, sheep 200, veterinarian 1 , barbers 2, total 567.** A proxy for how ridiculous some metrics may get. Up to the point in which the sum appears (567) we had a very good picture of the place. The sum killed it.

85. **When Compliance people, Quality people and Health and Safety people say 'the last thing we need is creativity.** 'The last thing we need is creativity' is a good line, but this is where the merit ends. Running a company on Stand-Up Comedy mode is both cheap and dangerous.

86. **Shock and awe communication campaigns de-scale quickly, they never scale up.** But create a tsunami of information and we love to get wet. Communication is not change. 'Smoking kills', 'Don't drink and drive' and 'Get the flu vaccine' don't need more billboards on highways.

87. **Rules of Viral Change™.** This compilation comes from several sources including *Viral Change™* (2006, 2008) *Homo Imitans* (2011) and *Mobilize! Masterclass* (2019), a 4+ hour and 28 chapter video masterclass that I have created and can be viewed at *vimeo.com/ondemand/mobilizemasterclass*

88. **The best ideas in conferences come during the break. The best conference is the one structured as a very long**

coffee break. The concept of Open Space Technology as a format for large group meetings was born from this simple observation. It was 1980. Still relevant.

89. **Everybody agrees the strategy in the meeting room. Everybody trashes the strategy in the toilets during the break.** My rule of thumb: rush to the toilets to be the first, hide in there and let people 'be honest'. You will learn a lot. Unfortunately, I only get the view of 50% of the population.

90. **The obsession with what is obviously measurable, in front of your eyes.** All sorts of cognitive biases, including availability heuristic, kick in when we focus on the immediately available or immediately recalled. These are part of our Applied Critical Thinking seminar.

91. **When recruiting, ask for examples of mistakes lived in previous employments.** Explore the concept of External vs Internal Locus of Control, if you are not familiar. Running an organization with 'external locus of control' people (it's not me, it's the system) is a serious health hazard. Avoid.

92. **Anything in a sentence before the word 'but' is bullshit.** Don't know who said that but surely a wise human being.

93. **A poor top leadership guarantees permission to get away with murder downstream.** It's a sad liability of leadership that a good one does not guarantee success downstream but a bad one most likely opens the doors for institutionalised mediocrity.

94. **Trust is key (and all the garbage of the paragraph).** Change the word trust or any other 'management thing' and you'll see the same. At the very best, we function on circular thinking with no problem, no red face, and believing we are smart. Openness is being authentic, authenticity needs honesty, honesty needs openness, and I will catch you back on authenticity soon. It's only a matter of time until you'll be back to the beginning.

95. **Elevator pitches. Nothing that needs explaining in an elevator, is worth explaining at all.** The term 'in summary' used to come after a long explanation. Now the 'in summary' is the explanation. The reality TV show *'Dragon's Den'*, that originated in Japan (*'Tigers of Money'*) and is now running in 30 countries has popularised pitching. Pitching is an art, so is the art of creating power lines and slogans. But surrendering to the elevator is a choice. Don't count on me. If you want my summary, come with me on the Orient Express.

96. **Some leaders have an open-door policy, by invitation only.** Openness, transparency, approachability, are like Henry Ford's 'any colour you want as long as it's black'.

97. **'Bottom-up' is not more workshops but at the bottom of the organization.** Sticking the term 'bottom up' to anything that has to do with involving employees has become a fashion and a term used to sound progressive and not a management dinosaur.

98. **Leadership is not a permanent Q&A session.** Some leadership models perpetuate the assumption that leaders know best and have all the answers.

99. **Culture is the company's petri dish.** I use this analogy systematically.

100. **M&A communication to all: 'we are going to create a new company with the best of each of us.'** Heard too often and seen too often. The consolidation of crap as a consequence of an M&A does not seem to me a terribly enlightening goal. Yet, this 'the best of us' always comes across as reassuring and encouraging for future merged citizens. There is a bit of arrogance of those going to merge with that attitude. I have never seen an M&A (and I have seen a fair number of them) that ends with a true sum of the best plus the best being truly outstanding. Maybe it's just my bad luck.

101. **To preach de-hierarchical-isation is to preach de-humanisation, not the opposite.** The reframing of hierarchy from problem to solution may not make me very popular but I believe that we have created so many antibodies that we have become a bit blind. I am very suspicious of the de-hierarchical-isation movement as a fashion on the catwalk of management.

102. **'Here we put people first. They are the first to go'.** It's not my cynical representation of reality. However, if you plan some layoffs, refrain from platitudes you may come to regret. Former chairman and CEO of Southwest Airlines, Herb Kelleher, was a master of the contrarian 'employees are first, customers are second'. The book *'Patients come second'* (2013) is a health care derivate.

103. **What people think and what people say are occasionally connected.** The best training is the one that teaches us to ask, 'what's the question behind the question?' and 'what is it that he is not saying?'

104. **'When the sea was calm, all ships alike; they show mastership in floating'.** Most of our established management practices and principles were created at a time of reasonable predictability in a more or less linear world. In that old world of management, complexity or chaos theory were an anecdote. In that old world, the 7 steps to change and 3 steps to anything made some sense. Today those approaches are as useful as plumbing expertise would be to perform a cardio triple bypass.

105. **Busy-ness is a semi-permanent state of continuous occupation that usually carries a high degree of self-importance.** At vice president level, busy-ness is flying around the world and shouting directions on an iPhone from airport lounges, never in the town you are supposed to be, always one before or one after. Phoning from a distance makes people very important, particularly when you can start the phrase with 'I am about to catch a plane to Singapore'. At not vice president level, busy-ness is to play vice president but without the airmiles and the gold card.

106. **Over-inclusiveness paralysis. Over-inclusiveness is always, always a sign of bad leadership.** Over-inclusiveness' own, unintended side effect is low trust. You need trust to let go and not be present in any single meeting or forum.

107. **4 targets to blame: (1) yourself, (2) others around you, (3) the system, (4) the global conditions.** Mary Douglas, a great British anthropologist who died in 2007, wrote on this and many other topics. I suggest her collection of essays *'Risk and Blame'* (1994)

108. **Process junkies hijack the territories of efficiency and destroy effectiveness.** The battle efficiency-effectiveness is not going away. Efficiency needs a strict process structure. Effectiveness (reaching great results beyond the predicted) does not ignore processes, but it's not a servant of them. 'Good management' preaches not to reinvent the wheel. My recommendation is not to go to the grave without having reinvented one or two.

109. **I hope you can see the slide from the back: always a very high probability that you can't.** All slides should be created at the back of a big room. Audio visual people should have optometrists on the payroll.

110. **'You can impress me with complete sentences.'** I have fully adopted the saying.

111. **Words are fingers pointing to the moon.** Read Julian Baggini's book *'How the world thinks'* (2019) for a real treat on how humanity uses different lenses to understand what is going on.

112. **'May all your teeth fall out except the one that gives you pain'.** I learnt of this in a (The) New York Times article referring to the outstanding book by Fintan O'Toole, *'The politics of pain'* (2019), about Brexit and new English nationalism.

113. **If you want to run a successful company, you need to have at least these four values: Respect, Integrity, Communication and Excellence. Enron did.** And its culture featured in numerous places as a model of this and that.

114. **An audience is not a community. Most communication systems create audiences.** A few questions in the Town Hall meeting do not create a community. They don't even represent 'employee voice'. Routine two-way dialogue is another matter. If online, if you are going to have an audience, make it multi-thousand.

115. **In any organization there are noise-amplifying people and noise-cancelling people.** Don't give leadership positions to noise amplifiers. Life is short.

116. **In a completely self-managed organization (if you ever see one) there are no bosses. But everybody is a competitor.** I used to be a reasonable fan of internal competition. Progressively I have come to see its problematic side. Today, I would put my money on collaboration. Or on an internal version of *coopetition*, a term that defines the collaboration between competitors to get shared benefits. Adam M. Brandenburger wrote the book as far back as 1997.

117. **Tao philosophy for management: To know what one does not know is best.** An injection of Taoism is much better than 20 off-sites with group facilitators and post-its. The *'those who know do not talk about it; those who talk about it do not know'* is a gem. Amazon has an entire list/category of 'Taoist Philosophy'. Tao Te Ching has been translated more than 250 times so English versions vary. Do a bit of digging before buying one.

118. **Large scale interventions are not small-scale ones repeated several times.** Physicist Albert A. Bartlett's famous quote about growth population applies to pretty much everything we do in life, including management practices: *'The greatest shortcoming of the human race is our inability to understand the exponential function'*.

119. **Management team composition should be 'by invitation', not by a given geographical position in the organizational chart.** It works extraordinarily well. Direct reporting does not mean an automatic seat at the management team level. Launched in *Disruptive Ideas* (2008) and part of the Seminar of the same title run by my teams.

120. **In a regatta (I am told) you win by making less mistakes than the boat that was going to win.** I did not know anything about regattas, let alone have any inclination for sporting analogies. (I am genetically unable to understand physical challenges, from sailing the Atlantic solo, to climbing dangerous mountains; attempts to rehabilitate me in the past have always failed). I changed my mind when one of my best CEO clients took her management teams boat racing. I learnt a lot (including the less mistakes thing). Thanks Louise Makin.

121. **We talk a lot about people needing to feel that the values of their company are consistent with their personal values. We know what we don't like, much more than what we do like.** Start by what is not acceptable, needs to be rejected, is inconsistent with 'your values', in order to get to the non-negotiable. We use this language ('non-negotiable behaviours') in our Viral Change™ programmes (and the rigidity annoys many people). I have a hard time understanding 'alignment of values'. I prefer 'compatible dreams'.

122. **Scientism is taking over management.** I have suggested elsewhere to read *'The tyranny of metrics'* by Jerry Z Miller (2018)

123. **My solution to a 'chicken and egg' problem is the omelette. Deadly serious about this.** Because I am fed up with the tyranny of the 'or'.

124. **There is a particular form of leadership that I really dislike. It's the one in which the audio and the video don't match.** And there is a lot of sync problems around. Years ago, we walked away from a prestigious project where the CEO was a regular of TV talks about values, but my team, negotiating the contract, were treated as third class citizens. I have never regretted it, but did not ask my bank manager's opinion either.

125. **If you were to discard all management practices and principles but could keep just one, this is it: fix**

accountabilities. Also, if you fix accountabilities, you may be fixing 'the structure' as well. An apparently loose and chaotic structure may be just what you need, provided accountabilities are fixed. Launched in *Disruptive Ideas* (2008) and part of the Seminar of the same title run by my teams.

126. **Machines work on feedback. Minds work on feed-forward.**
The feedback loop is not by any means the climax of calibration, control, adjustment, improvement...
Not for humans.

127. **Change is social, doing it together, a praxis.** The modern Kyoto Zen school is truly rich in observations. The Roman vs Greek comparison is very present in recent Taleb writings. The 'collapsing the distinction between knowing and doing' is of course on the Zen side.

128. **Autoimmune disease. Listing self-inflicted problems is not that hard for any savvy manager.** In fact, I ask clients to do this and create lists such as 'problems that do not exist, but we seem to love to have'; 'good problems to have'; 'little problems with the voice of big problems'; etc.

129. **Stop complaining about silos between divisions. Computer screens are the new silos.** Most structural solutions (amalgamation of divisions or groups) are a response to behavioural problems (e.g. lack of collaboration). Entire reorganizations, with hundreds of people disrupted, are triggered by very few people being the problem. The so-called Big Collaboration Problem between Marketing and Sales can actually be traced back to Peter, Head of Marketing, and Mary, Head of Sales. The rest have no problem but are forced to migrate with their screens. I believe that most silo problems have names and surnames.

130. **I have seen many corporate functions in large organizations that live in a bubble.** Years ago, we lost a significant project to be implemented in an affiliate of a world bank, precisely by being recommended by its own Global Organizational Development function, sucked into their abysmal reputation. Lesson learnt.

131. **Find gracious, generous people of character who want to make a difference.** Decouple titles and rank from the individual. One of the key success factors in our Viral Change™ programmes is that Viral Change™ project teams have no hierarchy within. Also, our communities of champions are hierarchy-free. Their membership is completely divorced from ranks in the system, even if those ranks still exist outside the borders of the Viral Change™ programme.

132. **'Studies show' that organizations which outperform have 5 strong values.** We are told that a few things are common in a particular type of, say, success. Never why the non-successful also have some of these things. The weekly discovery of unequivocal characteristics of something, which will enjoy a short fame (very short) and then will fade unceremoniously for another 'discovery', or another 'study, or another McKinsey report to take over, it's a fundamental characteristic of management thinking.

133. **To use a 'fixing mode' to change or to shape an organizational culture, is a bad idea.** Not many people get up in the morning thinking 'I am going to the office to fix the system', or 'to perform continuous improvement', or 'to rationalise processes for the innovation of the future'. Always be charitable with those who do, though. Building something new, better, stronger, future proofed, more advanced... That is much more attractive. Not done any 'study' here. If you are in culture change mode, abandon any fixing mental frame.

134. **Jeff Bezos' and Jack Welch's contributions to management thinking.** There are many management saints, some dead (Steve Jobs), some alive (Tom Peters). I have never understood the sainthood of Welch. I have always seen him as a monumental case study of what is wrong with traditional alfa-management. Welch died this year. Now his legacy will be scrutinized even more, and I don't think the balance will be positive.

135. **I profoundly dislike *nombrilisme*.** The poem *'Jamesian'* consists of two lines, *'their relationship consisted in deciding* *if it existed'*. It was written by Thom Gunn who died in 2004. I was introduced to it by the late John O'Donohue, Irish poet, philosopher, ex-priest, a figure that has significantly influenced my life. I am still a little angry with him for dying at 52.

136. **The best employee engagement programme is the one that doesn't exist because it is not needed.** Making 'employee engagement' work has always been called management. The fact that we needed to create an extra programme for it, tells you a lot about the strength of management itself.

137. **The entire Management theory and traditional MBA 'research' (...) contains the largest amount of bullshit'.** Since English is not my first language, I am entitled to use bullshit liberally. I repeat, traditional management theory and practice is a colossal house of cards. And I did not mention the word. Read Harry Frankfurt from Princeton's short essay *'On Bullshit'*. It can be found online. There is also the so called Brandolini's Law: *'The amount of energy needed to refute bullshit is an order of magnitude bigger than to produce it'.*

138. **'Meetings' and 'teams' are two different things. Team equals meeting, is a cancer.** See my *Disruptive ideas* (2008) book.

139. **The Employee Engagement industry has managed to reinforce a mechanistic worldview of the individual.** This sub-industry is totally dominated by an input-output model in which we discuss the nature of 'the feeding of the cows in order to obtain better milk'. The production model is simply wrong. It reduces the individual to a machine. It's immensely degrading. The 'better engaged employees produce better results' is shameful, lacks moral authority and trivialises the nature of work. But I will never win this one.

140. **The fundamental goal of the leader is to create 'agency'.** I believe that the old concept of 'agency', that is, confidence and ability to act for ourselves and being accountable for our own actions ('control our own destiny') should be at the core of any understanding of leadership's duties and engagement of people. Anything that blocks or impairs agency (paternalism, allowing victimism, destruction of identity) is cancerous. You'll pay for it.

141. **Digital Transformation is a label used by many people who could not even attempt to give you a definition.** For good angles, look into the Centre for the Future of Organization, Drucker School of Management, run by Roland Deiser, who, undeservedly, invited me to join as Fellow.

142. **Work on fixed term teams.** Launched in *Disruptive Ideas* (2008) and part of the Seminar of the same title run by my teams.

143. **The word obvious has its roots in 'standing in the way'.** I learnt this from Carlo Brumat many years ago when teaching at DUXX School of Business Leadership in Monterrey, Mexico, a wonderful experiment that died of poor business leadership.

144. **Value systems 'on the wall' are tired. They need at least some sort of desperate articulation.** I have found this pattern more than once. Value: integrity. Underneath, behaviours: openness and honesty'. Explanation: we need to be honest to have integrity, let's be open and speak up. I can't imagine how many man hours and consulting fees it took to get to that piece of management literature, and then converted into wallpaper.

145. **Produce two contradictory thoughts and let them fight. Accept that both may win.** F Scott Fitzgerald said that *'The test of a first-rate intelligence is the ability to hold two opposed ideas in mind at the same time and still retain the ability to function'*. This tension is at the core of good cognitive functioning and may be far more important than we think. In my Critical Thinking seminars, I encourage this forcibly and on specific topics.

146. **Drucker argued that what can't be measured can't be managed.** Drucker had lots of good things to say, but not this one. Read *'The Tyranny of Metrics'* (2018) by Jerry Z Muller for a rehabilitation programme from your armchair.

147. **Be private. Keep your private world secret. It's sacred.** You could watch my TEDx talk *'In praise of Borders'* (2014). Google knows about it. There I end with The Border Diet: (1) Have secrets; (2) Make yourself undiscoverable; (3) Take Pascal classes (alone with yourself in a room); (4) Keep stocks high, then give; (5) Practice silence; (6) Don't do anything (not even meditation, meditation is doing something); (7) Avoid trivia (mental pollution); (8) 'Your posting is not important to us'; (9) Reconcile with your borders; (10) Go to number 1. Amen.

148. **'Readiness' (to change, to risk taking, to maybe anything) is a red herring.** This is probably at the top of my most annoying statements, certainly for people who sell readiness.

149. **I spent my MBA, many moons ago, learning about the German car manufacturing industry.** I enjoyed my MBA. I was doing a top industry job at the time. I was also left by my ex-wife, abruptly, on my own with two teenagers. I became incredibly proficient at sourcing au pairs from Croatia on progressively shorter turnarounds, so Michael Porter and case studies about Volkswagen and Toyota were a walk in the park. And I mastered the writing of one single essay that looked like three different ones to three different lecturers. My final dissertation on competitor intelligence did not mention the word computer once.

150. **The best Employee Engagement Survey has only one question: Why are you still here?** They are called 'Stay Interviews' and I have no idea why they have not become popular. It's one of the greatest management ideas I have ever seen. Exit interviews are overrated.

151. **If you create lots of 'agile teams'.** Most of the non-agile practices I have seen recently are those coming from an Agile Programme. For all its merits, Agile has become an unavoidable label for people who bank on labels too much and who want to be seen as advanced. Kaizen, Six Sigma and others were here before. Organizations are trapped in the fashionable cultural necessity of 'doing Agile'. Once the certified people are in, the not too agile leaders don't have to do much. It's all done by the experts on post-its.

152. **In some organizations, all things seem well packaged, matters closed, structures are the answer to all the questions.** Perfect organizational structures are a sign of decay, without the 'when' fully spelt out.

153. **An enlightened and committed top leadership team does not guarantee an enlightened and committed organization.** We need to stop looking up. The top leadership is neither the reason for all successes or the cause of all dysfunctions. The organization is a system. Systems behave in funny ways and are able to function with some dysfunctional pieces.

154. **360 feedback is the great deceiver.** A 'culture of feedback' is always praised as superior. When feedback is institutionalised, the whole thing becomes mechanistic. Robotic processes deprived from real meaning. If 'feedback' is part of the daily, prosaic conversation, then you don't need the 360 Maoist system. Or any benign form with narrow angles (180 degrees etc). Incidentally my preferred angle is 45 degrees, which is the one you need to look at yourself in a mirror.

155. **The flipchart is the largest corporate graveyard of ideas. Their individual biographies are the Lost Scrolls of corporate memory.** I feel very sad for the flipchart. Always ready, always white, always welcome, then torn apart and forgotten. For a while, it was the host of innovation, wild ideas, proprieties, circles and arrows, unreadable statements and all our best intentions condensed in the 'top three of anything'. Then orphaned again, in the corner, thinner, forgotten, dead. RIP. I want to write a novel under the title *'The unauthorised biography of a flipchart'*. Would I get a grant from the History Society?

156. **The best resource management training is not taught in business schools: how to use and manage resources that**

you don't own. Teenagers and digital natives solved the problem very quickly. They saw their resources unlimited, unable to download them to a spreadsheet.

157. **Non-magic question: what are the goals and objectives?** Reframing questions is at the core of Critical Thinking training, something that we do in my company.

158. **A simple format about your culture to share or agree with your people.** These are examples of 'social algorithms', a concept, technique and application that we use in Viral Change™.

159. **At the end of the workday (...) 'the sunset must not find you still angry'.** Brought this here, out of so many days when I failed.

160. **'Smartphones are the new tobacco'.** The app Hold gives away rewards such as cinema tickets to students. I am told that, in Norway, more than 50% of the student population are today Hold users. You earn points by not using the smartphone. An idea apparently originated in Copenhagen Business School.

161. **This is the 'what' of Viral Change™ in a box.** My two books on Viral Change™ are *Viral Change™* itself and *Homo Imitans*. These days I recommend starting with the latter and going backwards, if there is any appetite left.

162. **Choose your problems before they choose you.** Yes, you can.

163. **List your competitors, then compare yourself with anybody not on that list.** In the old pioneering days of electronic payment (for example at the point of buying) the major telecom operators were watching each other and comparing advances between them. Busy on that daily exercise, they did not see Apple coming. Apple was not in the lists of telecoms operators.

164. **Giving people a voice implies that they don't have one.** Our language tricks us without noticing it. Similarly, 'lifting

people out of poverty' implies that they need a lift, they cannot do it by themselves. So, a philanthropic activity, for example, will be based upon the provision of the lift mechanics, not the enabling of people to lift themselves. People become lifted. If we did not pay attention to the language, nobody would ever see any problem with this.

165. **We have been taught, to the extreme of an unquestionable mantra, that we should not worry (and actually, should be pretty relaxed) about the things that are not under our control.** If you cared to list the things that are not under your control and decide not to worry or touch, you would be out of anything from citizenship, politics, education of your kids, social change, or fighting injustice. Yes, doable, but (here we go, Rabbi Hillel, who is said to have lived for 120 years and died in 10CE) *'If I am not for myself, who will be for me? If I am not for others, what am I? And if not now, when?* Three questions, three flipping questions.

166. **Beware of people telling you that their work is 'evidence-based' (medics, scientists, engineers).** I am prepared to have a discussion with people who warn me that they are 'evidence-based' only after they prove to me that they have read *'Fooled by randomness'* (2007) by Nassim Taleb. Then we talk, so I can shorten the conversation by 90%.

167. **Benchmarking is a race against somebody who has already won.** Benchmarking was invented when one could actually stop time. I remember the times of thick binders and benchmarking subscriptions. I never understood the point, but it was a requirement by executives who wanted to look rational.

168. **The most important management question is 'what is the question?'.** I tend to ask people to write the answer down first in private. Then, when we share, we discover we have as many different answers as participants, but we were just prepared to go ahead assuming we all had the same in mind. Last time I did it with a team of R&D leaders, and I asked them to write down the end of the sentence 'the role of R&D is...' we ended up with as many different answers as members. At least half of the answers were irreconcilable with each other.

169. **The only way to address differences between us, is to find the common and shared spaces and then work from that territory first.** I love Obama's recent talk to 'woke' people: *"The world is messy. There are ambiguities. People who do really good stuff have flaws. People who you are fighting may love their kids and share certain things with you."*

170. **I must have an on-off switch on trust in my brain. It's never in between.** I have this big problem: people I love can never go wrong even if they tried. It has its own liabilities, but the pleasure is incommensurable.

171. **If you have a choice to (re)design an organization on the basis of 'who needs to do what' or 'who needs to know what'.** Organizational design, as usually practiced, is quite irrational. Mostly it's based upon a military concept of command and control. It is only when alternative designs based upon different criteria are let to compete with each other conceptually, that one can see the pros and cons of each and the kind of trade-offs one is prepared to make.

172. **The following qualify for early retirement on compassionate grounds due to their poor health, in some cases terminal illness.** Are we still friends despite my list?

173. **'A man without a smile can't open a shop', the Chinese proverb says.** It may be bumper sticker material but, hey, there are so many things one could stick.

174. **The current shelf life of a Best Practice is 5 minutes, and it's been a while since I last checked.** 'Best Practices' found a very welcoming home in management thinking and praxis because it brought a scientific flavour, let alone validation, to the table. Last time I attended a Best Practices meeting in my previous corporate life, people called 'best practice' to anything they have done. Everything was a Best Practice, and what a fantastic feeling to have when the company does nothing but Best Practices. That your competitors did the same was a small detail to consider. Best Practice exercises are the best Catch Up shows.

175. **The 'sorry-I-have-to-go-to-another meeting' people should always be encouraged to go straight to that one and bypass yours.** I call them The Visitors. Always hopping from one place to another, always busy, never in one place long enough, self-important, nomadic managers, corporate Tuaregs, worthy of a job in the Sahara affiliate.

176. **We want the organizational flexibility of Lego. We recruit for the rigidity of a jigsaw.** For those who want both: you need to at least settle for a percentage of re-configurable Lego structures in the company. Leading jigsaw organizations is leading prisons, even if they look like golden cages. And you always, always drop that piece in the corridor. Finding the replacement is exhausting.

177. **In this meeting, any statement related to an answer, or a position after brainstorming, or at the time of making a decision, must not start with 'it depends'.** The question is, what if it did not depend? Contingency models of leadership, organizational structure, decision making, basically say that 'you get what you need' and 'you do what you need to do' depending on the situation. Situational leadership, in particular, preaches 'it depends'. Trouble is, it is very easy to mistake context (some things may depend on it) for wild relativism (nothing is ever fixed or absolute), or even worse a permanent cheaply available way out of any commitment. The latter is what we usually see in many organizations.

178. **We often lack the discipline of questioning. Perhaps we lost it in kindergarten.** I heard years ago about a Japanese executive, I wish I remember who, who said *'I am now of seniority that I can only ask questions, I have no answers'.*

179. **Non magic: what is the latest intelligence and new data? Magic: what's the story?** The magic, non magic collection would go for ever. I have always hated the sanitised corporate language. The exaggerated and disruptive language of

Ronald D Laing, a British psychiatrist who died in 1989, father of the then called 'antipsychiatry movement' and a figure who all of us, standard and medicalised psychiatrists in white coats, hated at that time, because it was 'the right thing to do', said in his complaining and critical mode: *Gone is any language of joy, delight, passion, sex, violence. The language is that of the boardroom.'* The last bit stuck in my head.

180. **Peer power: If managers say, 'safety is first', the impact may be relative (...) If my peer says, 'safety is first', I'm beginning to pay attention.** Peer-to-peer is the strongest source or engine of change and mobilization inside any organization.

181. **My kind of people are those who, in front of a crap and lousy process, make things happen first and then find the energy to tackle the crap process and change it.** I have not met many but, wow, what a joy and delight when one of these turns up in your life!

182. **Some organizations should have a sign at the front door quoting Dante's Inferno: 'Abandon all hope when entering here'.** Corporate environments are cross-contaminating 'cultures' (as in a petri dish, where things grow). What it grows is largely created by the day to day interactions of people. Some environments produce fluidity, hope or a sense of worth. Others are Dante's places. The late C. K. Prahalad, great mind and author, who died in 2010 also had a term for terrible environments: 'Calcutta in summer'.

183. **Why on earth do some people start their CVs with 'I am a thought leader' or 'I am an influencer'? Seriously.** People mistake what is perfectly reasonable for others to say about you, and what you say of yourself.

184. **The only skill needed in a dialogue is not to hear what the other says but to interpret it: what is behind his question?** For 'this is not working', read 'I don't like it'. For 'I don't understand it' read 'I don't want to understand'. Maybe.

THE FLIPPING POINT

It needs practicing. It gets better with practice. Above all my rule of thumb is never react and respond immediately with an obvious answer.

185. **The industry of Employee Engagement says that companies with high employee engagement are more successful (...) My view is that success creates employee engagement, not the other way around.** The book *The Halo Effect* (2014) by Phil Rosenzweig opened my eyes to this. I would put this book in the list of obligatory reading to anybody in management. The subtitle of the book is explicit: *'and the Eight Other Business Delusions That Deceive Managers'*. Rosenzweig quotes the case of the UK retailer Marks and Spencer, a company which at some point scored at the top in employee engagement rankings. Then a terrible year in business performance came up and employee engagement scores went down significantly. Not a single iota in benefits, programmes, employee care, or anything had changed. Just abysmal market performance.

186. **I have met a big boss who wrote memos, long hand, for his secretary to type and send by normal mail.** I used to collect oddities until I discovered that they were normalities. Today we have normalised being untruthful and people with severe personality disorders hold high offices so, frankly, this is a flipping world.

187. **I've met many top leaders in my life whose greatest merit seemed to be avoiding mistakes.** In my previous corporate life, we used to call them 'chronic survivors'. And they seemed to belong to a nomadic tribe that went from company to company, always a step higher in the ladder, immune to big reorganizations. Most left corporate life at a not particularly old age, very wealthy, to become venture capitalists, ephemeral consultants or chairmen of obscure start-ups.

188. **Victimism (adopting a victim role) is one of the most powerful toxic conditions that any organization can have within it.** The best recent work in this area comes from

Bradley Campbell and Jason Manning, who wrote the book *'The Rise of Victimhood Culture: Microaggressions, Safe Spaces, and the New Culture Wars'* (2018). It's focused on American colleges, but the ideas can be extrapolated. For a good summary on the topic google it in *The Atlantic Magazine* (2015). I have a book project on this topic applied to organizational life.

189. **I wish I could respect people not in a hurry but, unfortunately, I never seem to manage to meet them.** They are always behind, catching up, fighting yesterday's battles, but earning a salary like anybody else.

190. **When the physicist Wolfgang Pauli was shown a paper by a young colleague, he described it as 'not even wrong'. Not even wrong!** Try that! It does not get better when you call out a piece of bullshit.

191. **A top leadership team should not be composed of people, who are representing their functions or business units in the company, reporting to the boss.** There is a magic threshold in organizational life at which a management team stops representing their troupes and starts representing *into* their troupes. That is the magic point when collective leadership starts. If this happens, for whatever mechanism, you are incredibly lucky.

192. **Social media is a colossal echo chamber where all cognitive processes are surrendered to one single driver: confirmation bias.** The only solution is periodical rehab. Make yourself offline for a while. Read books with physical pages. Send handwritten letters to friends.

193. **A world class movement in Health Care is trying to switch the emphasis from 'what is the matter?' (your pain, symptoms, difficulties) to 'what matters to you?'.** This is a magic shift of great consequences. We have incorporated the thinking into our Viral Change™ programmes.

194. **The Saint Francis School of Management is at the top of**

my personal ranking. **'Preach the Gospel all the time; when necessary use words.'** In many organizations, the motto seems to be *'preach the thing all the time, and if necessary, preach again, don't stop preaching, preaching is good. They need to get it'*.

195. **We have an obsession with the homogeneous organizational model and an aversion to combining different models under one roof.** Taleb says *'I am, at the Fed level, libertarian; at the state level, Republican; at the local level, Democrat; and at the family and friends level, a socialist'*.

196. **When organizations grow, their systems and processes grow (...) At some point, managing the internal complexity becomes a greater problem than managing the complexity of the environment.** I feel very strongly that these lenses explain a lot of self-inflicted problems. My solution: (1) stay in beta; (2) stay small or break up in small units [Dunbar's number of 150? Bezos's teams of one pizza feeding?]; (3) Never try to reproduce in small what a big company is.

197. **Revere the past, then move forward and leave it to the archaeologists.** *'Those who cannot remember the past are condemned to repeat it'*, said Jorge Santayana, Spanish philosopher. He didn't say *'stay there and admire the problems'*.

198. **Culture is the difference between 30 people making a decision in 30 days, or 3 people making the same decision in 3 days.** I use lots of these examples to show that culture is 'hard', not 'soft'. Anybody with a calculator can see it.

199. **People with all the answers are overqualified for any job.** I probably heard this from Tom Peters many moons ago, I don't know, but it stuck in my mind big time.

200. **Cultures are not created by training.** Fundamental premise of the Viral Change™ approach.

About the Author:
Leandro Herrero

I am the CEO of The Chalfont Project, an international firm of organizational architects, and the designer of its products and services in the areas of large scale, behavioural change (Viral Change™), collective leadership and smart organizational designs. I have written several books in these areas and I am also, if lured into it, an international speaker on organizational culture and leadership topics.

Today, I am proud to say that Viral Change™, the flagship of The Chalfont Project, has impacted on more than a quarter of a million employees so far, in both the private and public sectors, across geographies.

Before this wonderful 20 year adventure, with a fantastic team, I spent many years as a hands-on leader in several world class companies, in areas such as pharma R&D, commercial health care roles and health economics. That means, I have been on the other side of the fence. And, before that, I was a practicing clinical psychiatrist, treating patients and teaching in the university at the same time. I wasn't one of those couch types of psychiatrists. I wore lots of white coats. And I wrote 3 books as well.

I also have an MBA, which I completed at the same time as working in the pharmaceutical industry and it helped me to transition from medical doctor (basically an alien) to manager (basically an indigenous species). It also allows me to make bad jokes about MBAs, probably its most useful outcome...

I am a Fellow member of several management bodies keeping alive some appearance of faithful tribalism.

I have lived in the United Kingdom for more than 30 years now and escape to my home country, Spain, with my family as much as I can in search of the Mediterranean light.

I am above all a European citizen, therefore an immigrant in Britain, a wonderful place where I have always felt at home. In a way, Brexit has been my own unwelcome flipping point.

Drawing on his behavioural sciences background and acute observations from his extensive body of work as an Organizational Architect, Leandro Herrero, consultant, author and international speaker, seeds this thinking in his Daily Thoughts blog and in his other books.

The Leader with Seven Faces:
Finding your own ways of practicing leadership in today's organization

After all the books written about leadership, you'd think we know a thing or two about leadership. However, nothing seems to be further from the truth.

The Leader with Seven Faces provides a novel approach to leadership where the questions to ask (about what leaders say, where they go, what they build, care about, do, how they do it and 'what' they are) take priority over producing 'universal answers'.

For anybody interested in leadership of organisations... and in seeing things through a new pair of glasses.

New Leaders Wanted: Now Hiring!
12 kinds of people you must find, seduce, hire and create a job for

A small percentage of the workforce has the key to success. A selected group of managers make all the difference. But what are the skills these people have that enable them to create business success?

The job advertising pages don't often describe those new skills. There is a tendency to play safe and look for people with a conventional set of skills and a proven track record. However, to get spectacular success, you need an 'internal engine' of people who think and behave differently. Who are these people? Where could they be? Do I have them already or do I need to find them? You cannot ignore these questions and your number one priority should be to find these people.

New Leaders Wanted explores those new skills and new approaches to reality and will guide you in your search to find those people.

Disruptive Ideas
10+10+10=1000: the maths of Viral Change™ that transform organizations

In a time when organisations simultaneously run multiple corporate initiatives and large change programmes, *Disruptive Ideas* tells us that - contrary to the collective mindset that says that big problems need big solutions - all you need is a small set of powerful rules to create big impact.

In his previous book, *Viral Change™*, Leandro Herrero described how a small set of behaviours, spread by a small number of people could create sustainable change. In this follow-up book, the author suggests a menu of 10 'structures', 10 'processes' and 10 'behaviours' that have the power to transform an organisation.

These 30 'ideas' can be implemented at any time and at almost no cost; and what's more... you don't even need them all. But their compound effect will be more powerful than vast corporate programmes with dozens of objectives and efficiency targets...

Viral Change™

The Alternative To Slow, Painful and Unsuccessful Management of Change in Organizations

Lasting change in modern organizations has less to do with massive 'communication to all' programmes and more with the creation of an internal epidemic of success led by a small number of people focused on a small set of non-negotiable behaviours.

This is the basis for *Viral Change™*, an unconventional approach to the management of change for any company.

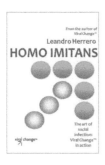

Homo Imitans

The art of social infection: Viral Change™ in action

Managing sustainable change is mastering the art of social infection, both in the micro- and macro-social world. In *Homo Imitans*, Leandro Herrero shows us how to achieve this through his successful *Viral Change™* approach.

Homo Imitans explores the power of social copying and social imitation and explains how to orchestrate change by using that largely untapped power.

It shows you how to create social epidemics of success based on the five pillars of change: behaviours, influence, networks, stories and distributed leadership.

Cultural change in organizations and the macro-social world is *Viral Change™*. Cultures are not created by training or information cascades. Behaviours create culture, not the other way around. *Homo Imitans* explains why and how.

However: Work Could Be Remarkable

There are two types of people in organizations: 'Therefore People' and 'However People'. The 'Therefore People' have all the pieces of reality in front of them and conclude, "We must do X". The 'However People' have the same pieces, but conclude, "It looks like we should do X, however, we could also explore Y or Z. We always have options". This is a book about ideas, about people, about work in organizations. It is born out of the belief that work can be remarkable. 'However' thinking is Leandro Herrero's path to uncovering possibilities.

In each of the short chapters of the book, he encourages us to look at contrarian or unconventional views, to reframe obvious questions, to be brave and to challenge the many default positions that are usually well-entrenched. Organizations are in desperate need of an epidemic of 'However'. This is a 'However' book. It is an invitation to think critically and to engage in work with the be-lief that it can be remarkable.

Leandro Herrero writes a daily blog 'Daily Thoughts' at leandroherrero.com/subscribe-to-the-blog

To be part of this community subscribe now.

Follow us on:

@LeandroEHerrero, @chalfontproject, @viralchange

WE ARE YOUR ORGANIZATIONAL ARCHITECTS

If you want to build a remarkable organization or challenge your status quo, we are your organizational architects. If you need the best leadership, if you want a collaborative environment, if you want to master change or instil radical management innovation: we promise you will have them. Work with us. We won't tell you things just because you want to hear them.

We will advise you, work with you and we will make a difference. We don't do 'small difference' – if this is what you have in mind, don't hire us. We work with people with ambition, who see possibilities, who have a sense of urgency and who want to make a difference in their worlds – teams, leaders, companies, society. Also, we don't do misery. Pain is sometimes inevitable, but misery is always a choice. (Not ours though, life is short).

Warning: we have a bias for behaviours in everything we do. Others may ignore them in favour of processes or structures, but for us there is no change of any kind unless there is behavioural change. So, talk to us.

www.thechalfontproject.com
uk-office@thechalfontproject.com
+44 1895 549158